HOW TO PREVAIL IN EVERY BATTLE OF LIFE

ALSO FROM REVIVAL TODAY

Financial Overflow

Dominion Over Sickness and Disease

Boldly I Come

Twenty Secrets for an Unbreakable Marriage

How to Dominate in a Wicked Nation

Seven Wrong Relationships

Everything a Man Should Be

Understanding the World in Light of Bible Prophecy

Are You Going Through a Crisis?

The 20 Laws that Govern the Financial Anointing

35 Questions for Those Who Hate the Prosperity Gospel

The Art of Spiritual Warfare

Help for Your Darkest Time

Seven Reasons Your Church Will Never Have Revival

Who Told You You're in a Season of Waiting?

How to Prevail in Every Battle of Life

Books are available in EBOOK and PAPERBACK through your favorite online book retailer or by request from your local bookstore.

HOW TO PREVAIL IN EVERY BATTLE OF LIFE

JONATHAN SHUTTLESWORTH

Without limiting the rights under copyright(s) reserved below, no part of this publication may be reproduced, stored in or introduced into a retrieval system, or transmitted in any form or by any means (electronic, mechanical, photocopying, recording, or otherwise) without the prior permission of the publisher and the copyright owner.

The content of this book is provided "AS IS." The publisher and the author make no guarantees or warranties as to the accuracy, adequacy or completeness of or results to be obtained from using the content of this book, including any information that can be accessed through hyperlinks or otherwise, and expressly disclaim any warranty expressed or implied, including but not limited to implied warranties of merchantability or fitness for a particular purpose. This limitation of liability shall apply to any claim or cause whatsoever whether such claim or cause arises in contract, tort, or otherwise. In short, you, the reader, are responsible for your choices and the results they bring.

The scanning, uploading, and distributing of this book via the internet or any other means without the permission of the publisher and copyright owner is illegal and punishable by law. Please purchase only authorized copies, and do not participate in or encourage piracy of copyrighted materials. Your support of the author's rights is appreciated.

Unless otherwise noted, all Scripture quotations are taken from the *Holy Bible, New Living Translation* (NLT). Copyright © 1996, 2004, 2007, 2013 by Tyndale House Foundation. Used by permission of Tyndale House Publishers, Inc., Carol Stream, Illinois 60188. All rights reserved.

Scripture quotations marked KJV are taken from the *King James Version* (public domain).

Scripture quotations marked NKJV are taken from the New King James Version (NKJV). Copyright © 1982 by Thomas Nelson, Inc. Used by permission. All rights reserved.

Scripture quotations marked JUB are taken from the *Jubilee Bible 2000* (JUB). Copyright © 2000, 2001, 2010 by Life Project. Used by permission.

Scripture quotations marked AMPC are taken from the *Amplified Bible, Classic Edition* (AMPC). Copyright © 1954, 1958, 1962, 1964 by The Lockman Foundation. Used by permission.

Copyright © 2025 by Revival Today. All rights reserved.

Release Date: February 2025
Paperback ISBN: 978-1-64457-626-7
Hardcover ISBN: 978-1-64457-627-4

Rise UP Publications
www.riseUPpublications.com

CONTENTS

Introduction   7

Part I
GOD'S PLAN FOR YOUR VICTORY

Chapter 1   11
The Blessing

Chapter 2   19
The Sacrifice

Chapter 3   23
The Curse

Chapter 4   35
The Provision

Chapter 5   43
The Enemy

Part II
YOUR DEFENSE STRATEGY

Chapter 6   57
Live Holy

Chapter 7   71
Be Spirit-Led

Chapter 8   75
Resist

Chapter 9   83
Understand Your Identity

Part III
YOUR OFFENSIVE WEAPONS

Chapter 10   99
Jesus the Rod: Your Source of Power

Chapter 11   107
Your Mouth

Chapter 12   121
Fasting & Prayer

Chapter 13   127
Touch

Chapter 14   131
Praise

Part IV
FINAL LESSONS

Chapter 15   141
13 Lessons from the Book of Job

Chapter 16   159
Seven Facts About Apostle Paul

Chapter 17   167
Visualize Your Victory

Afterword   173
Notes   175
Author Photo   176
About the Author   178

INTRODUCTION

When you receive salvation, you become born again. You're no longer like everyone else. You're redeemed into an enviable destiny that others will find attractive. People should not look at your life and think, 'Oh wow, isn't that a shame? They're a Christian now.' No, they'll ask, "Good Lord, what happened to you?"

When my wife was saved at sixteen years old, almost all her friends and extended family were unsaved, including those in her household. At the time of this writing, we've been married for eighteen years, and in that time, everyone in her family has come to accept Jesus: cousins, family, and friends. They follow our ministry because they've seen what becoming a Christian has done for her life. They've watched our marriage grow strong as we raise a blessed child and fulfill what God said in His Word: *"I will bless you. I will multiply you. I will multiply your seed. And through you, all the nations of the earth will be blessed"* (Genesis 22:17-18). Being a Christian didn't lead my wife and I to bankruptcy and food kitchens—unless it was to feed other people.

God doesn't take people down; He takes people up. He takes the beggar from the dunghill and sets him among princes (1 Samuel 2:8). That's the God I serve. He doesn't want you to meander through life in hopes that

INTRODUCTION

one day it'll all be worth it when you make it to Heaven. God will make serving Him worthwhile right now if you do your part. Meditate on His Word, day and night. Take it seriously as a matter of life and death. Make a concerted effort to read your Bible, and let it point out any flaws in your life. Don't read it like a typical American who takes offense and disagrees with what it says. God doesn't work on your terms; you work on His.

Imagine if God the Father appeared to Joshua and said, "Listen, you've been in My presence now, all your worries are over. See you in Heaven." Joshua would have exclaimed, "I saw God!" and that would have been the end of it, but that's not how God works. He appeared to Joshua and instructed him to never let the Bible out of his sight.

Believe the Word and speak it. Don't wait for it to happen. Put your feet on it. For New Testament believers, your feet are your words. Let the Word flow out of your heart and out of your mouth, because by *"the produce of his lips will a man be satisfied"* (Proverbs 18:20).

You must adopt a certain attitude to produce victory in your life. If you assume a religious posture and carry yourself like the third guy from the left on the evolutionary chart, you won't achieve victory. God's instruction to us was to *"Be strong and be very courageous"* (Joshua 1:7). Refuse to fear. Jesus never coddled people who feared. He rebuked fear because fear is a spirit. Never be afraid, dismayed, or discouraged. Don't allow yourself to feel these emotions.

Your mind is your servant, not your master. When you cast down thoughts that are against God's Word, you're using the power God gave you to eject what you don't want out of your life and receive what you do want into your life. You are not a powerless victim of circumstances. When God's Word comes alive in you, God makes you the head and never the tail. You're in charge.

Life doesn't control your destiny. You have dominion, but you must abide by God's Word to control the outcome of your life and prevail in every battle that comes your way.

PART I
GOD'S PLAN FOR YOUR VICTORY

CHAPTER 1

THE BLESSING

"If you fully obey the Lord your God and carefully keep all his commands that I am giving you today, the Lord your God will set you high above all the nations of the world. You will experience all these blessings if you obey the Lord your God. Your towns and your fields will be blessed. Your children and your crops will be blessed. The offspring of your herds and flocks will be blessed. Your fruit baskets and breadboards will be blessed. Wherever you go and whatever you do, you will be blessed. The Lord will conquer your enemies when they attack you. They will attack you from one direction, but they will scatter from you in seven! The Lord will guarantee a blessing on everything you do and will fill your storehouses with grain. The Lord your God will bless you in the land he is giving you. If you obey the commands of the Lord your God and walk in his ways, the Lord will establish you as his holy people as he swore he would do. Then all the nations of the world will see that you are a people claimed by the Lord, and they will stand in awe of you."

— DEUTERONOMY 28:1-10

The Bible says all the nations of the world will stand in awe of you for the great things God will do. You will not be pitied by the world. The Lord will give you prosperity in the land.

Prosperity is not a concept invented in Tulsa, Oklahoma in the 1970s; it's from the Bible. God said, *"The Lord your God will soon bring you into the land he swore to give you when he made a vow to your ancestors Abraham, Isaac, and Jacob. It is a land with large, prosperous cities that you did not build"* (Deuteronomy 6:10). Prosperity is not God meeting your needs—that's survival. Prosperity is God supernaturally empowering you to meet the needs of a hurting world. I'm writing this to help you do that.

> "The Lord will give you prosperity in the land He swore to your ancestors to give you, blessing you with many children, numerous livestock, and abundant crops. The Lord will send rain at the proper time from His rich treasury in the heavens and will bless all the work you do. You will lend to many nations, but you will never need to borrow from them."
>
> — DEUTERONOMY 28:11-12

The Word says, *"You will lend money to many nations but will never need to borrow"* (Deuteronomy 15:6). Ninety-nine percent of people will say "Amen" to that statement but will never let it lay hold of their spirit. You'll rarely find someone who's accomplished something significant within the body of Christ that wasn't bank-funded. God doesn't want you to make monthly payments. God wants people to make monthly payments to you.

God promised to make you the head and not the tail and give you prosperity. Not once did He mention giving you favor with someone who has prosperity so they can loan you money at a six percent interest rate. The Bible says God will enrich you and make you great. Your land will be blessed. Your homes will be blessed. Your family will be blessed, and no one but God will be able to take credit for it.

There's little wonder why those in the nation's upper echelons don't have any interest in attending church. They feel superior to God every time those who represent Him ask people like them for help. Why would they need our God when they're the ones who loaned us the money to build His church? But a new generation of Christians is forming. A generation of people who don't have their hand out to the world for help because God has raised them to meet the needs of their hurting world.

You will never arrive at a destination you don't know exists. If you think it's normal to struggle, or that marriage is supposed to be rocky, children are supposed to do drugs and fall away from serving the Lord, even though you raised them in church, and you'll never have enough money —that's exactly what your life will entail.

Proverbs 23:7 says, *"As a man thinketh in his heart, so is he."* Your biblical reality begins with the renewal of your mind and a change of heart through the Word of God. The Bible isn't a fantasy. It's God's will for you. If you believe His Word, God will empower you to achieve the plans He has for you.

> "The Lord will give you prosperity in the land he swore to your ancestors to give you, blessing you with many children, numerous livestock, and abundant crops. The Lord will send rain at the proper time from his rich treasury in the heavens and will bless all the work you do. You will lend to many nations, but you will never need to borrow from them. If you listen to these commands of the Lord your God that I am giving you today, and if you carefully obey them, the Lord will make you the head and not the tail, and you will always be on top and never at the bottom. You must not turn away from any of the commands I am giving you today, nor follow after other gods and worship them."
>
> — DEUTERONOMY 28:11-14

How can you interpret, "*Always the head, never the tail, always on top, never at the bottom*" as mountains and valleys? Yet, that is what most of us have been taught in church.

> 'The Lord will cause you to be defeated by your enemies. You will attack your enemies from one direction, but you will scatter from them in seven! You will be an object of horror to all the kingdoms of the earth."
>
> — DEUTERONOMY 28:25

Most Christians know the scripture, "*They shall come out against you one way and flee before you seven ways*" (Deuteronomy 28:7). But God also said that if you don't serve Him, when you attack your enemy *you'll* end up running from them seven ways.

> "Moses my servant is dead. Therefore, the time has come for you to lead these people, the Israelites, across the Jordan River into the land I am giving them. I promise you what I promised Moses: 'Wherever you set foot, you will be on land I have given you— from the Negev wilderness in the south to the Lebanon mountains in the north, from the Euphrates River in the east to the Mediterranean Sea in the west, including all the land of the Hittites.' No one will be able to stand against you as long as you live. For I will be with you as I was with Moses. I will not fail you or abandon you."
>
> — JOSHUA 1:2-5

People will try to stand against you, but they'll never be successful. You can have perpetual victory and expel failure from your life.

> "No one will be able to stand against you as long as you live. For I will be with you as I was with Moses. I will not fail you, and I'll never abandon you. Be strong and courageous, for you are the one who will lead these people to possess all the land

I swore to their ancestors I would give them. Be strong and very courageous. Be careful to obey all the instructions Moses gave you. Do not deviate from them, turning either to the right or to the left. Then you will be successful in everything you do."

— JOSHUA 1:5-7

GOD'S PROMISES TO YOU

1. *"Wherever your foot will tread, you'll be on land that I've given you."* (Joshua 1:3)
2. *"I will make you successful in everything you do."* (Joshua 1:8)
3. *"No one will ever be able to stand against you as long as you live."* (Joshua 1:5)

Living by these three passages of Scripture from Joshua 1 makes it hard to fail at anything. It's not some weird religious delusion to think this way. I'm not sitting in a dark hole somewhere while everything falls apart around me, claiming to be blessed in the spirit realm. I'm *visibly* blessed and successful.

In Deuteronomy chapter twenty-eight, the Bible says the heathen will *see* it and know that you're a people claimed by God, and they will stand in awe of you. The Jewish people are blessed. Even their enemies admit they're blessed. Israel's enemies fire rockets at them and can't hit them with a single missile. The Israelis don't bother to cancel school when enemy missiles aim at them because the blessing of God is on them. God protects and fights for them. The Bible says the blessing of God is what makes this a reality.

The same blessing the Jewish people enjoy belongs to everyone in Christ Jesus. *"There is no longer Jew or Gentile, slave or free, male and female. For you are all one in Christ Jesus"* (Galatians 3:28). When God told Abraham, *"I will bless you, and through you, all the nations of the earth will be blessed,"* He was referencing Jesus' arrival to Earth from the line of Abraham to be a blessing for every tongue, tribe, nation, and race.

Today, this blessing is visible in Israel. The Jewish people comprise 0.2 percent of the world's population yet produce twenty-two percent of the Nobel laureates. How is 0.2 percent of the population producing a quarter of the people dominant in their field? By the blessing of God, that's how. It's the same blessing passed down from Abraham through Jesus, and now it's upon all who put their faith in Jesus Christ.

Galatians 3:9 says, *"So all who put their faith in Christ share the same blessing Abraham received because of his faith."* That's what God gave us—He gave us His blessing.

> "Be strong and courageous, for you are the one who will lead these people to possess all the land I swore to their ancestors I would give them. Be strong and very courageous. Be careful to obey all the instructions Moses gave you. Do not deviate from them, turning either to the right or to the left. Then you will be successful in everything you do. Study this Book of Instruction continually. Meditate on it day and night so you will be sure to obey everything written in it. Only then will you prosper and succeed in all you do."
>
> — JOSHUA 1:6-8

This book is a roadmap to achieving prosperity and success in everything you do. It will show you how to apply God's Word, and when you do, He will give you success and prosperity in every area. God never leads you backward. God always leads forward, and when you follow the Holy Spirit, He never leads you to failure. These are not arbitrary rules that God gave us for fun. He always has a destination in mind.

If Joshua 1:6-8 were the only verses in the Bible and the only agreement God made with us, I would embrace Christianity for that benefit alone. Forget Heaven and everything else God promised for just a second. Imagine having guaranteed success and prosperity in everything you do. Imagine being granted a way to always rise above your enemies. Count me in! Like Sanballat and Tobiah, when they rose against Nehemiah, God will strip your enemies of any power to succeed against you and empower you to move forward and take the land. That's a deal worth taking.

God is not in Heaven ticked off, threatening to kill everyone who doesn't follow His commands. He told you what to do to dominate on Earth. No enemy or weapon formed against you will prosper. Any tongue that rises up against you, you will condemn (Isaiah 54:17). No one has the power to shut you down.

Nikita Khrushchev, the former premier of the USSR, made it his mission to bury The Church of Jesus Christ in the USSR. But they buried Nikita Khrushchev, and The Church in Russia is the third fastest-growing church in the world. God won't allow any enemy to keep you down. In the same way that the lions couldn't touch Daniel, and the fiery furnace had no power over Shadrach, Meshach, and Abednego, your enemies have no power over you.

When they threw Paul in prison, he was a guest in the jailer's jacuzzi within hours, and a church was started as a result of his imprisonment. When Paul was broken out of prison, everyone's chains fell off and every prison door came open. That's the kind of power God put in you. People in the Bible provoked God to action by presenting an offering of thanks to God for His last provision and to prove to Him that their heart was involved in their giving. It was an expression of their love for God.

> Then they entered into a covenant to seek the Lord, the God of their ancestors, with all their heart and soul. They agreed that anyone who refused to seek the Lord, the God of Israel, would be put to death—whether young or old, man or woman. They shouted out their oath of loyalty to the Lord with trumpets blaring and rams' horns sounding. All in Judah were happy about this covenant, for they had entered into it with all their heart. They earnestly sought after God, and they found him. And the Lord gave them rest from their enemies on every side.
>
> — 2 CHRONICLES 15:12-15

When you serve God, He gives you rest from your enemies. Total victory is scriptural. A life of ups and downs is not biblical. You were created to go from glory to glory, victory to victory, and strength to strength. God promised you would always be the head, never the tail, always on top, never at the bottom. He promised to make you successful in everything you do. Wherever your feet tread, you'll be on land that He has given you. No one will be able to stand against you as long as you live. God didn't just promise victory; God promised victory after victory.

CHAPTER 2

THE SACRIFICE

But those who depend on the law to make them right with God are under his curse, for the Scriptures say, "Cursed is everyone who does not observe and obey all the commands that are written in God's Book of the Law." So it is clear that no one can be made right with God by trying to keep the law. For the Scriptures say, "It is through faith that a righteous person has life." This way of faith is very different from the way of law, which says, "It is through obeying the law that a person has life." But Christ has redeemed us from the curse pronounced by the law. When he was hung on the cross, he took upon himself the curse for our wrongdoing. For it is written in the Scriptures, "Cursed is everyone who is hung on a tree." Through Christ Jesus, God has blessed the Gentiles with the same blessing he promised to Abraham, so that we who are believers might receive the promised Holy Spirit through faith.

— GALATIANS 3:10-14

The Bible doesn't say Christ *will* redeem us. It doesn't say Christ *is* redeeming us. It says Christ *has* redeemed us. If someone tells you, "You're free," the first thing you should want to know is what you're free from. The Bible tells you that you've been set free from all the curse of the law. *"When he was hung on the cross, he took upon himself the curse for our wrongdoing. For it is written in the scriptures, 'Cursed is everyone who is hung on a tree'"* (Galatians 3:13).

When Jesus came in the fullness of time, God orchestrated the method of Jesus' death. That's why Jesus wasn't killed by French guillotine, firing squad, or hanging. He wasn't stoned or beaten to death—He was crucified on a cross because it is written in the Old Testament: *"Cursed is anything that hangs on a tree"* (Deuteronomy 21:22–23). When Jesus hung on the cross, the Bible says He became the curse for your wrongdoing. Every curse that should have been laid on you was laid on Christ.

Death by crucifixion was supposed to take at least three days because it caused victims to suffocate slowly, but Jesus died in only six hours. Death came quickly for Jesus because as He hung there, He bore the spiritual curse of sin along with every sickness and disease of mankind—heart disease, cancer, AIDS, and every disease that would ever exist. He died so quickly the executioners accused him of faking His death. To fulfill the prophecy that would free us from the curse, the soldiers pierced His side instead of breaking His legs like they did the other two criminals crucified with Him (John 19:31-37). The curses that Satan meant for us were placed on Christ and it didn't just have spiritual ramifications, it physically killed Him. The Devil fought so hard to invalidate Jesus' sacrifice for our salvation that he influenced the Pharisees to disseminate a lie saying His disciples rescued Him from the tomb and told everyone He rose from the dead (Matthew 28:11-15).

T.L. Osborn once said, "It's illegal for the Devil to put on you what's already been laid on Christ Jesus." You don't double-pay for your groceries. You don't double-pay for a speeding ticket. If someone pays your bill, it doesn't have to be paid again. Jesus used His blood as payment for a debt He didn't owe because we owed a debt we couldn't pay.

Sin separated us from God, so God placed the sin that separated us from Him on Christ. Jesus became our substitution on the cross. When Jesus took our sins on the cross, God could no longer look at His Son. He turned His face away from Christ, but Christ's sacrifice has enabled Him to look at us. That's what caused Jesus to say, *"My God, my God, why have you forsaken me?"* (Matthew 27:46).

Jesus' sacrifice was foreshadowed by a type in the Old Testament:

> Then the people of Israel set out from Mount Hor, taking the road to the Red Sea to go around the land of Edom. But the people grew impatient with the long journey, and they began to speak against God and Moses. "Why have you brought us out of Egypt to die here in the wilderness?" they complained. "There is nothing to eat here and nothing to drink. And we hate this horrible manna!" So the Lord sent poisonous snakes among the people, and many were bitten and died. Then the people came to Moses and cried out, "We have sinned by speaking against the Lord and against you. Pray that the Lord will take away the snakes." So Moses prayed for the people. Then the Lord told him, "Make a replica of a poisonous snake and attach it to a pole. All who are bitten will live if they simply look at it!" So Moses made a bronze snake and attached it to a pole. Then anyone who was bitten by a snake could look at the bronze snake and be healed!
>
> — NUMBERS 21:4-9

Jesus said in John 3:14, *"As Moses lifted up the serpent in the wilderness, so the Son of Man must be lifted up."* Jesus likened what happened physically with Moses and the Israelites to what would take place spiritually through His death on the cross. Then He said, *"I will give you authority to trample on serpents and scorpions"* (Luke 10:19). The Devil appeared as a serpent in the Book of Genesis, and we can overcome any invisible serpent that seeks to steal, kill, and destroy because Jesus became the serpent for us. He was raised on a cross, just as the bronze serpent was raised on a pole.

His sacrifice enabled all who come to Him to be healed and live, just as the Israelites followed the command of Moses, looked at the serpent, and lived by faith.

The Word of God is rich and awesome. Christ didn't die on a cross solely to secure your place in Heaven, He carried your sin, sickness, disease, and curse. The curse that afflicted you left when you turned to face Him and recognized that Christ took your place. That was the complete work and purpose for Jesus' death on the cross.

When He hung on the cross, He took upon Himself the curse for your wrongdoing. The next time you read Galatians 3:13-14, insert your name. Make it personal. Tell Him, "Thank you, Jesus, for taking my curse."

CHAPTER 3

THE CURSE

Now that you know you're redeemed from the curse of the law, let's examine the curse Christ has redeemed you from. Both the blessing and the curse are outlined in the Book of Deuteronomy. Before we review the curse, let's review the blessing.

> "If you fully obey the Lord your God and carefully keep all his commands that I am giving you today, the Lord your God will set you high above all the nations of the world. You will **experience** all these blessings if you obey the Lord your God: Your towns and your fields will be blessed. Your children and your crops will be blessed. The offspring of your herds and flocks will be blessed. Your fruit baskets and breadboards will be blessed. Wherever you go and whatever you do, you will be blessed. The Lord will conquer your enemies when they attack you. They will attack you from one direction, but they will scatter from you in seven! The Lord will guarantee a blessing on everything you do and will fill your storehouses with grain. The Lord your God will bless you in the land he is giving you. If you obey the commands of the Lord your God and walk in his ways, the Lord will establish

you as his holy people as he swore he would do. Then all the nations of the world will **see** that you are a people claimed by the Lord, and they will stand in awe of you."

— DEUTERONOMY 28:1-10

You'll notice I've emphasized the words *experience* and *see* because they indicate something that manifests in the visible realm. You don't have to pretend to be blessed while driving a beat-up car or as you walk to take the bus. When you believe, the blessing is actualized in your life.

> "The Lord will give you prosperity in the land He swore to your ancestors to give you, blessing you with many children, numerous livestock, and abundant crops. The Lord will send rain at the proper time from His rich treasury in the heavens and will bless all the work you do. You will lend to many nations, but you will never need to borrow from them. If you listen to these commands of the Lord your God that I am giving you today, and if you carefully obey them, the Lord will make you the head and never the tail, and you will always be on top and never at the bottom."

— DEUTERONOMY 28:11-13

These verses illustrate how to realistically prevail in every battle of life. God didn't claim He would *usually* scatter your enemies when they attack you, but sometimes He'd allow you to get your butt kicked. He didn't state that you'd *sometimes* be the head and sometimes the tail, most of the time on top, *occasionally* at the bottom. That's not in the Bible. *"You'll always be the head, never the tail, always on top, never at the bottom. You must not turn away from any of the commands I'm giving you today, nor follow after other gods and worship them."* That's the blessing for obedience.

We've all had agreements pop up on our computers that read, "Click to agree before you continue," followed by 13 pages of jargon in small font. No one reads it before clicking "Agree." But when it comes to my life, this is one instance where I want to read the fine print. When I learned that I was redeemed from the curse of the law, I wanted to see, specifically what I was redeemed from. I wanted to know what Jesus redeemed me from that no longer has access to my life. You're about to read the fine print of an agreement. What's written in these verses cannot be accessed by those who aren't in Christ. This is the reason those in your life who don't know the Lord live such hard lives. This curse is on all of mankind until they come to Christ, but once you come to Christ, what Jesus took in your place cannot be put back on you unless you allow it.

In the next few verses, the curse Christ has redeemed us from is described at length. If you were to read this passage without knowing that according to Galatians 3:13, you've already been redeemed from this curse, these would be the most depressing verses in the entire Bible. But as a believer, none of this applies to you. This describes what your life would have looked like had Christ not redeemed you.

> "But if you refuse to listen to the Lord your God and do not obey all the commands and decrees I am giving you today, all these curses will come and overwhelm you: Your towns and your fields will be cursed. Your fruit baskets and breadboards will be cursed. Your children and your crops will be cursed. The offspring of your herds and flocks will be cursed. Wherever you go and whatever you do, you will be cursed."
>
> — DEUTERONOMY 28:15-19

Robert Young, a respected scholar and Scottish Bible translator, explained there is no causative tense in the original Hebrew for this portion of scripture. The New Living Translation cycles from *"The Lord will send"* to *"These curses will come."* But it should have always been translated as *"These curses will come"* because God doesn't curse you for not serving Him. The same way God doesn't have to make you wet when you're standing in a river, deciding to live without God, is a decision to live where curses flow. The Bible tells you what naturally occurs outside of God. He doesn't have any sickness in Heaven to send to you. He doesn't have poverty to send to you. He has streets paved with gold. Heaven is filled with abundance and joy, but when you're in the Devil's domain, he has access to do whatever he wants to do to you.

> "The Lord himself will send on you curses, confusion, and frustration in everything you do, until at last you are completely destroyed for doing evil and abandoning me. The Lord will afflict you with diseases until none of you are left in the land you are about to enter and occupy. The Lord will strike you with wasting diseases, fever, and inflammation, with scorching heat and drought, and with blight and mildew. These disasters will pursue you until you die. The skies above will be as unyielding as bronze, and the earth beneath will be as hard as iron. The Lord will change the rain that falls on your land into powder, and dust will pour down from the sky until you are destroyed."
>
> — DEUTERONOMY 28:20-24

Notice the Bible lists disease as a curse. It isn't mentioned among the blessings for obedience, it's mentioned among the curses for disobedience. God doesn't place sickness on people. It doesn't matter if you use a sickness to lead every nurse in the hospital to the Lord, your sickness didn't come from God. He may take what the Devil meant for bad and use it for good, but He didn't make you sick. He redeemed you from all the curse of the law, and sickness is a curse.

If you were to fly over Israel, you'd be amazed to see that it looks like a garden in the middle of a wasteland. As soon as you leave Israel and fly over other Middle Eastern nations, there's nothing—I mean nothing.

When I flew back from India on a clear day, I followed along on the digital map in business class. I could see the sparse terrain as we flew over the Middle East region. Every twenty minutes we'd fly over a town, I'd look it up on Wikipedia, and learn the populations were all around two hundred people. They were like a group of people living on a rock. Nothing grows there, it's just sand. Then there's Israel, this little nation the size of New Hampshire, where they grow watermelon, guava, and all types of produce that is grown in fertile nations like Puerto Rico. They export gold and diamonds all over the world.

God said, if you don't serve Him, the rain would turn into sand. You can see it. Israel is tangible proof of the difference between the blessing and the curse.

> "The Lord will cause you to be defeated by your enemies. You will attack your enemies from one direction, but you will scatter from them in seven! You will be an object of horror to all the kingdoms of the earth. Your corpses will be food for all the scavenging birds and wild animals, and no one will be there to chase them away. The Lord will afflict you with the boils of Egypt and with tumors, scurvy, and the itch, from which you cannot be cured. The Lord will strike you with madness, blindness, and panic. You will grope around in broad daylight like a blind person groping in the darkness, but you will not find your way. You will be oppressed and robbed continually, and no one will come to save you. You will be engaged to a woman, but another man will sleep with her. You will build a house, but someone else will live in it. You will plant a vineyard, but you will never enjoy its fruit. Your ox will be butchered before your eyes, but you will not eat a single bite of the meat. Your donkey will be taken from you, never to be returned. Your sheep and goats will be given to your enemies, and no one will be there to help you. You will watch as your sons and daughters are taken away as slaves. Your heart will break for them, but you won't be able to help them. A foreign nation you have never heard about will eat the crops you worked so hard to grow. You will suffer under constant oppression and harsh treatment. You will go mad because of all the tragedy you see around you. The Lord will cover your knees and legs with incurable boils. In fact, you will be covered from head to foot. The Lord will exile you and your king to a nation unknown to you and your ancestors. There in exile you will worship gods of wood and stone! You will become an object of horror, ridicule, and

mockery among all the nations to which the Lord sends you. You will plant much but harvest little, for locusts will eat your crops. You will plant vineyards and care for them, but you will not drink the wine or eat the grapes, for worms will destroy the vines. You will grow olive trees throughout your land, but you will never use the olive oil, for the fruit will drop before it ripens. You will have sons and daughters, but you will lose them, for they will be led away into captivity. Swarms of insects will destroy your trees and crops. The foreigners living among you will become stronger and stronger, while you become weaker and weaker."

— DEUTERONOMY 28:25-43

Have you noticed that when a historically large church begins to turn away from God and accept false doctrine and liberal theology, its congregation shrinks? Oftentimes to help increase revenue, it will allow other churches to rent their space. As outside groups come in, the original congregation that departed from God continues to shrink, but those who honor God and win souls grow larger until they buy the church and kick the original owners out. That's just a small example of what God said will happen nationally.

This dynamic is currently sweeping through Europe. Islamic Jihadists have infiltrated Germany, and rather than address the violence, the German government urged its female population to refrain from jogging at night.

It's happening in England, too. The nation that sent preachers all over the world is now filled with empty churches and is being taken over by a foreign religion. The former mayor of London has openly stated that terrorism is a natural part of living in a large city, but it's not natural, it's spiritual. Nations will either serve God and be blessed or depart from Him and watch as foreigners move in and drive out their citizens from the land they once enjoyed. This is not fake. This is real.

> "They will lend money to you, but you will not lend to them."
>
> — DEUTERONOMY 28:44

Borrowing is a curse. Being dependent upon other people to finance your life is not a blessing, it's a curse. It's not a sin, but instead of looking at life in terms of what is and isn't a sin, you should determine how to produce the best outcome according to God's Word. If you're wondering if it's a sin to take a loan, you're asking the wrong question. If God said you can lend and not borrow and described borrowing as part of the curse, then you should have no desire to borrow. Don't settle for the minimum, strive for the maximum blessing and separate yourself from every aspect of the curse.

REVIVAL IS AMERICA'S ONLY HOPE

> "They will be the head, and you will be the tail! If you refuse to listen to the Lord your God and to obey the commands and decrees he has given you, all these curses will pursue and overtake you until you are destroyed. These horrors will serve as a sign and warning among you and your descendants forever. If you do not serve the Lord your God with joy and enthusiasm for the abundant benefits you have received, you will serve your enemies whom the Lord will send against you. You will be left hungry, thirsty, naked, and lacking in everything. The Lord will put an iron yoke on your neck, oppressing you harshly until he has destroyed you. The Lord will bring a distant nation against you from the end of the earth, and it will swoop down on you like a vulture. It is a nation whose language you do not understand, a fierce and heartless nation that shows no respect for the old and no pity for the young."
>
> — DEUTERONOMY 28:44-50

Islamic Jihadists have long attempted to infiltrate America. We are right at the door of this being fulfilled. That's why revival is so important. It's not about having a nice altar service. Revival is the difference between America being overrun by people who are hellbent on seeing this great nation destroyed, or our nation being restored back to God. How could you more aptly describe the agenda that has plagued our government for so long? From Islamic Jihadists to George Soros, their goal is to see our country's Christian roots ripped out. America's only chance is for people to rise up, preach the Gospel, put the fire of God in people, and stand in the gap.

> "Its armies will devour your livestock and crops, and you will be destroyed. They will leave you no grain, new wine, olive oil, calves, or lambs, and you will starve to death. They will attack your cities until all the fortified walls in your land—the walls you trusted to protect you—are knocked down."
>
> — DEUTERONOMY 28:51-52

The Department of Homeland Security can't protect America from the curse. There is no physical defense against the spiritual curse. You could enlist every male in the United States and declare martial law, but it wouldn't matter. If America turns from God, it's over. But if America turns toward God, the nation will see the blessing of God sweep through it once again.

> "The siege and terrible distress of the enemy's attack will be so severe that you will eat the flesh of your own sons and daughters, whom the Lord your God has given you. The most tenderhearted man among you will have no compassion for his own brother, his beloved wife, and his surviving children."
>
> — DEUTERONOMY 28:53-54

When a father walks out on his family, and his kids can't get ahold of him, it's a spiritual curse. I'm sure you've seen news stories of mothers and fathers committing unspeakable acts of violence against their own children. You've probably wondered, 'How can someone do something like that?' It's demonic. You'll either experience blessings or curses.

> "The most tender and delicate woman among you—so delicate she would not so much as touch the ground with her foot—will be selfish toward the husband she loves and toward her own son or daughter. She will hide from them the afterbirth and the new baby she has borne, so that she herself can secretly eat them."
>
> — DEUTERONOMY 28:56-57

When you read the above passage of Scripture in America, people automatically assume it could never happen, but if you visit third-world nations, you'll find this happens daily. Preachers in America don't take these things seriously because they think it will never reach this point. Americans must wake up. The Devil didn't randomly decide to take it easy on America and unleash hell in other parts of the world. The strength of The Church of the Lord Jesus Christ has kept the Devil from taking hold here. If believers in The Church disarm themselves, the Devil will lay waste to the nation, but we refuse to allow this to happen, in Jesus' name.

> "If you refuse to obey all the words of instruction that are written in this book, and if you do not fear the glorious and awesome name of the Lord your God, then the Lord will overwhelm you and your children with indescribable plagues. These plagues will be intense and without relief, making you miserable and unbearably sick."
>
> — DEUTERONOMY 28:58-59

These verses perfectly describe the average American family that doesn't serve the Lord. They're overwhelmed with problems because it's part of the curse.

> "He will afflict you with all the diseases of Egypt that you feared so much, and you will have no relief. The Lord will afflict you with every sickness and plague there is, even those not mentioned in this Book of Instruction, until you are destroyed. Though you become as numerous as the stars in the sky, few of you will be left because you would not listen to the Lord your God. Just as the Lord has found great pleasure in causing you to prosper and multiply, the Lord will find pleasure in destroying you. You will be torn from the land you are about to enter and occupy. For the Lord will scatter you among all the nations from one end of the earth to the other. There you will worship foreign gods that neither you nor your ancestors have known, gods made of wood and stone! There among those nations you will find no peace or place to rest. And the Lord will cause your heart to tremble, your eyesight to fail, and your soul to despair. Your life will constantly hang in the balance. You will live night and day in fear, unsure if you will survive. In the morning you will say, 'If only it were night!' And in the evening you will say, 'If only it were morning!' For you will be terrified by the awful horrors you see around you. Then the Lord will send you back to Egypt in ships, to a destination I promised you would never see again."
>
> — DEUTERONOMY 28:60-68

God will allow you to oppose His promise for your life. Many people believe that whatever God wants to happen will come to fruition no matter what. That's not true according to these verses. If you don't participate by obeying God and holding up your end of the covenant, God said you'll return to the land He brought you from in ships, despite

His promise that you'd never return. You decide whether to participate in God's plan for your life.

> "There you will offer to sell yourselves to your enemies as slaves, but no one will buy you."
>
> — DEUTERONOMY 28:68

The curse of the law described in Deuteronomy chapter 28 is not read from many pulpits. That's why most Christians don't understand what they've been redeemed from. But when you understand that Jesus took the entire curse upon Himself and that nothing written from verses 15 through 68 applies to you, it becomes a very joyous passage of Scripture.

When you combine the revelation in Galatians 3:9 with God's promise in Deuteronomy 28, you have a clear scriptural outline for the areas of life in which you can expect victory.

CHAPTER 4

THE PROVISION

Now that you understand the ethereal concept of victory, let's consider practical victory. When God promised to give you rest from all your enemies, what enemies did He mean? When He said He'd give you success, what practical ways will He grant you success?

ARENAS OF CONTINUOUS VICTORY

1. Mental Health

Deuteronomy 28:28 says part of the curse is being stricken with madness, blindness, and panic. The Bible says, *"God has not given us a spirit of fear but of love, power, and soundness of mind"* (2 Timothy 1:7). A sound mind is a blessing, an uncontrolled mind is a curse, and Christ redeemed us from all the curse of the law.

Part of the blessing of Abraham is a sound mind. Part of the curse of the law is panic attacks and anxiety. It says at the end of Deuteronomy 28 that you'll be overcome by all the horrors around you, but as a believer, that's not your portion. Now you can declare:

I am redeemed from all mental disorders.

2. Marriage

Deuteronomy 28:30 says, *"You will be engaged to a woman, but another man will sleep with her. You will build a house, but someone else will live in it."*

Recently, I passed by a house with a pastor friend of mine. He told me the man who once owned the house lost it to his ex-wife in a divorce. Now she's remarried and lives there with her new husband. That's an example of the curse the Bible refers to.

There are professional athletes who woke up at 5 AM every morning to train since the age of five to obtain a high level of success and build their dream homes. Then they allowed sin to enter their lives and cheated on their wives. Even with a prenuptial agreement, they had to pay to suppress all the sordid stories from going public, and they lost the homes they had worked so hard to build. Their sin enabled other men, who never woke up early to train, to swing open the French doors of their homes like Gaston from *Beauty and the Beast*, wearing a plush robe and living comfortably in the houses they worked hard to build. But that will never be your story because, as a believer, you have victory in marriage.

3. Children

Deuteronomy 28:32 says, *"You will watch as your sons and daughters are taken away as slaves. Your heart will break for them, but you won't be able to help them."* The inability to control your children is part of the curse. Watching as outside forces turn them away from the principles and values you raised them to uphold is part of the curse.

But I'm not under the curse. My child will serve the Lord more when she's fourteen than she did when she was five. These passages show you that life is not left to chance. *"I've set before you blessings and curses. Oh, that you would choose life that you and your descendants might live"* (Deuteronomy 30:19). You can choose to live under the blessing. I made my choice. How about you? Can you declare:

I'm not under the curse. I am redeemed. My children are blessed.

4. The Work of Your Hands

According to the curse described in Deuteronomy 28:38, *"You will plant much but harvest little."* Working hard and having no money is part of the curse. The sociology field uses the term "working poor" to describe this phenomenon. Not everyone living in the inner city is on welfare, sitting around playing video games all day. Many people work two or three jobs, but still have no money, and can't afford to move out of the projects. The Bible says under the curse, you'll work hard, but you'll never enjoy the increase of your labor.

Every time I see someone in one of my meetings who's over sixty and sick, I think of this curse. They worked hard their whole life, but when it was time to enjoy the fruit of their labor, the Devil stole the opportunity from them. The redemption of Christ allows you to enjoy the fruit of your labor. No sickness will take it. No lawsuit will take it. Every devourer that the Devil uses to take your harvest is cursed. You are blessed, in Jesus' name. Declare it:

 I'm not under the curse. I am redeemed. I will enjoy the fruit of my labor.

5. Redemption from All Forms of Lack

According to the curse described in Deuteronomy 28:48, *"You will serve your enemies and be left hungry, thirsty, naked, and lacking in everything."* The majority of the verses that describe the curse deal with scarcity, inability to collect your harvest, hunger, thirst, and want of all things. Being in want and need is part of the curse. Jesus redeemed us from *all* the curse. If you don't serve the Lord, you'll be left wanting in every area. If the Lord is your Shepherd, you shall not lack (Psalm 23:1). Hallelujah! You can shout:

I'm not under the curse. I am redeemed.

You are redeemed from poverty, lack, scarcity, and from having to borrow instead of lend. You are the lender and not the borrower, the head and not the tail.

6. Sickness and Disease

Deuteronomy 28:61 says you have been redeemed from *"Every sickness and every plague which is not written in this Book of the Law."* It doesn't matter what new disease they invent this fall; God has already made provision for it.

I've already lived through several things that were supposed to wipe the world out—Bird Flu, Pig Flu, Asian Flu, Mad Cow Disease, Ebola, Zika, and Covid. Where are these diseases now? Exactly. I refuse to fear anything. The Lord is my light and my salvation.

How can anyone not believe in healing when the Bible says that every sickness and disease, even those not mentioned—fever, inflammation, blight and mildew, tumors, scurvy, the itch from which you cannot be cured—are part of the curse and Christ has redeemed us from all the curse?

Lift your right hand to God and say: "Thank you, Father, that I've been redeemed from every sickness and disease, even those not mentioned in the Bible. Christ took it in my place. I don't have to take it at all. He took all my sickness. He carried away all my disease. He's not *going* to do it. He *did* it already. I am redeemed. I am free, in Jesus' mighty name."

Begin to thank God with your mouth! Thank Him that your last bout of sickness and disease will be the last bout you'll ever have, in Jesus' name.

7. Plagues

The Bible says in Deuteronomy 28:59 that *"these plagues will be intense and without relief."* In the King James Version, it says, *"Plagues of long continuance."* Things that stick with you and won't go away are a curse.

When Jesus saw a man who had been crippled for thirty-eight years, He knew how long he had been that way and went over and asked, *"Would you like to get up?"* It was a curse, and it made Jesus angry. Jesus was so upset by it that He didn't wait for the crippled man to come to Him; He approached the man and asked him if he would like to be healed.

There was a woman who had been bent over for eighteen years. Jesus said, *"Why should this daughter of Abraham, whom Satan has bound, have to suffer one more day?"* (Luke 13:16). Jesus never told anyone to wait. Jesus never told anyone it was their season to suffer through sickness and disease. Plagues of long continuance are part of the curse, and Christ has redeemed us from all the curse of the law.

Victory in God is not the ability to wave a flag and blow a shofar, even though your wife has left you, your kids don't serve the Lord, and you don't have a ride to church. That's a pretend victory, and it reminds me of 1 Samuel 17 when the Israelite army would shout and make battle cries. Then, as soon as Goliath came, they all retreated to their camp. Fake victory is useless. For many people, that's what church is like. They experience victory in church, but when they go outside for six and a half days, they get their rear ends kicked by the Devil. But that's not true of you in Jesus' name.

GOD GAVE YOU DOMINION OVER:

1. Sin – *"Sin is no longer your master, for you no longer live under the requirements of the law. Instead, you live under the freedom of God's grace"* (Romans 6:14).
2. Death – *"The soul that sinneth, it shall die"* (Ezekiel 18:4 KJV)
3. Sickness – *"Also every sickness, and every plague, which is not written in the book of this law, them will the Lord bring upon thee, until thou be destroyed"* (Deuteronomy 28:61). We were under the curse of the law. Every sickness in existence, and every sickness that's not mentioned in this book of the law is part of the curse.
4. Hardship – *"The way of the transgressor is hard"* (Proverbs 13:15 KJV),

5. The Devil – *"Ye are of your father the devil, and the lusts of your father ye will do"* (John 8:44). The Devil and his demons once had dominion over us.
6. Poverty – *"All thy trees and fruit of thy land shall the locust consume"* (Deuteronomy 28:42). Lack of any kind is part of the curse of the law.
7. Sorrow – *"Many sorrows come to the wicked, but unfailing love surrounds those who trust the Lord"* (Psalm 32:10).
8. Failure – *"You will attack your enemy from one direction, but you'll run in seven directions."* (Deuteronomy 28:25). Nothing ever works out.
9. Fear – *"Because God's children are human beings—made of flesh and blood—the Son also became flesh and blood. For only as a human being could he die, and only by dying could he break the power of the devil, who had the power of death. Only in this way could he set free all who have lived their lives as slaves to the fear of dying"* (Hebrews 2:14-15).

The more specific you are about your dominion, the greater your dominion will be. Equip yourself with the understanding of your dominion and ensure you know how to apply it to every aspect of your life. Not only are you free from everything on that list, you have dominion over those things. You have power in the Word of God.

People think they need prayer, but they're wrong. They need power, and the source of the power they need comes from an understanding of God's Word. Thank God that you're understanding this today. Not only are you *free* from sin, death, sickness, hardship, the Devil, poverty, sorrow, failure, and fear, you have *dominion* over sin (Romans 6:14). You have *dominion* over death (Matthew 10), you have *dominion* over sickness (Matthew 10). You have *dominion* over hardship. Your life isn't hard. Surely goodness and mercy will follow you all the days of your life (Psalm 23:6).

The Devil wants you to remain bound to your identity as a sinner because being a sinner causes you to identify with things that are part of the curse, causing you to make allowance for them in your life. But when you understand the sinner is dead and you're now a new creature, you realize what does and doesn't belong to you. You can freely declare:

I have dominion over the Devil. I'm not only free from him, I have dominion over him. I have dominion over poverty.

The blessing of the Lord makes a man rich. You're not only free from poverty, you operate and swim in the riches of God. You have dominion over sorrow (Proverbs 10:22). *"Many sorrows come to the wicked, but unfailing love surrounds those who trust the Lord"* (Psalm 32:10). You have a different portion than the world. You've been redeemed out of this world. You have dominion over the things that are in this world. You have dominion over failure, and you will have good success and prosper in all you do (Joshua 1:8). The last failure you saw will be the last failure you ever see.

You have been freed from the fear of dying (Hebrews 2:14-15). When you understand your dominion, overwhelming victory is produced in the same way you exhale carbon dioxide. It just exudes from you because it comes from your root in the Word. *"Whatsoever is born of God overcomes the world. This is the victory that overcomes the world, even our faith"* (1 John 5:4). For you to receive this dominion, you must be born again. You can't just listen to Bible teachings; Christ must live inside you. He said, *"Behold, I stand at the door and knock. If any man hears My voice and opens the door, I will come in and share a meal with him as friends"* (Revelation 3:20).

CHAPTER 5

THE ENEMY

Anytime you attempt to move forward, there will be opposition. I've never denied the reality of opposition. Challenges are normal, but it's unscriptural to be defeated. Address your opposition as Peter did when he was arrested and not the way James handled it. When James was arrested, there was no record of The Church doing anything, and James died. When they arrested Peter, The Church prayed, and an angel of the Lord broke Peter out of prison. Not only did the angel rescue Peter from jail, but all the guards were killed in the process. Then, while the king who had Peter arrested was giving a speech, an angel of the Lord struck him, and he was consumed from the inside out.

> Whosoever digs a pit shall fall therein, and he that rolls a stone, it will return upon him.
>
> — PROVERBS 26:27 (JUB)

When Peter was arrested, the angel broke him out of prison. Even then, it wasn't over.

> At dawn there was a great commotion among the soldiers about what had happened to Peter. Herod Agrippa ordered a thorough search for him. When he couldn't be found, Herod interrogated the guards and sentenced them to death.
>
> — ACTS 12:18-19

Not only did God deliver Peter after they prayed, but everyone guarding Peter died in his place.

> Now Herod was very angry with the people of Tyre and Sidon. So they sent a delegation to make peace with him because their cities were dependent upon Herod's country for food. The delegates won the support of Blastus, Herod's personal assistant, and an appointment with Herod was granted. When the day arrived, Herod put on his royal robes, sat on his throne, and made a speech to them. The people gave him a great ovation, shouting, "It's the voice of a god, not of a man!" Instantly, an angel of the Lord struck Herod with a sickness, because he accepted the people's worship instead of giving the glory to God. So he was consumed with worms and died. Meanwhile, the word of God continued to spread, and there were many new believers.
>
> — ACTS 12:20-24

Either you receive a revelation that overthrows the attack of the Devil against The Church, or the power of the Devil will overthrow The Church. There's a huge difference between the Syrian church and the church in Texas, just like there's a massive disparity between the church in England and the church in Florida. One fights and the other doesn't.

The Bible doesn't just demonstrate God's promise of deliverance; it highlights deliverance *and* the destruction of those who would try to harm you. Deliverance is in the Book of Acts, and it hasn't died out. God didn't suddenly become passive after the resurrection of Jesus

Christ. He still destroys those aligned against His children, just like He did for Abraham.

Abraham knew people wanted to kill him. He knew he had a beautiful wife, and his enemies would kill him to get to her. So, he told the king that his wife was his sister. When the king took Abraham's wife into his harem, God visited the king and told him to return her or face the consequences. Without any prompting from Abraham, the king came to him and asked, "Why didn't you tell me this was your wife? I don't want to see your God again. Take her back. If I do anything else that upsets you, let me know so I can make it right." God was Abraham's protector. No one had any babies while Sarah was within that harem—a curse came on all the people.

> End the evil of those who are wicked, and defend the righteous. For you look deep within the mind and heart, O righteous God. God is my shield, saving those whose hearts are true and right. God is an honest judge. He is angry with the wicked every day. If a person does not repent, God will sharpen his sword; he will bend and string his bow. He will prepare his deadly weapons and shoot his flaming arrows. The wicked conceive evil; they are pregnant with trouble and give birth to lies. They dig a deep pit to trap others, then fall into it themselves. The trouble they make for others backfires on them. The violence they plan falls on their own heads.
>
> — PSALM 7:9-16

> Oh let the wickedness of the wicked come to an end; but establish the just: for the righteous God trieth the hearts and reins. My defence is of God, which saveth the upright in heart. God judgeth the righteous, and God is angry with the wicked every day. If he turn not, he will whet his sword; he hath bent his bow, and made it ready. He hath also prepared for him the instruments of death; He ordaineth his arrows against the persecutors. Behold, he travaileth with iniquity, and hath conceived mischief, and brought forth falsehood.

> He made a pit, and digged it, and is fallen into the ditch which he made. His mischief shall return upon his own head, and his violent dealing shall come down upon his own pate.
>
> — PSALM 7:9-16 (KJV)

The Bible says, *"The Lord killeth and the Lord maketh alive"* (1 Samuel 2:6). There are two sides to God. He loves His children, and He loves the lost, but those who make it their business to destroy people, God calls wicked, and the Bible says the Lord is angry with them every day (Psalm 7:11). That's still true today. It didn't end after The Resurrection. The way the Gospel is preached on American television, you would think God lost the battle after The Resurrection.

When a US Senator unconstitutionally demanded that ministries turn over their donor records to the United States Senate, Kenneth Copeland looked into the camera while filming his show and said, "Senator Grassley, you can have those documents when you pry them from my cold dead hand. You don't have any legal right to take them." He opposed government overreach, and the whole thing went away because he took a stand. Everyone else was preparing to hand over their records. There were hundreds of ministers on the government's list. If the separation of Church and State is breached, it's over; the government will sanction those who can preach and those who can't preach.

What you don't confront, you'll never conquer. Whatever you don't resist will always remain. Begging God won't make anything happen. You must open your mouth and speak the Word.*"...every tongue that rises up against you thou shalt condemn"* (Isaiah 54:17). You don't *pray* for deliverance; you *preach* deliverance. *"The Spirit of the Lord is upon me because He has anointed me to preach deliverance"* (Luke 4:18). That means you proclaim, under the unction of the Holy Spirit, what God said belongs to you, and you curse everything aligned against your advancement.

Chapter after chapter, the Bible provides examples of what happens when wicked men challenge His anointed.

> Afterward they traveled from town to town across the entire island until finally they reached Paphos, where they met a Jewish sorcerer, a false prophet named Bar-Jesus. He had attached himself to the governor, Sergius Paulus, who was an intelligent man. The governor invited Barnabas and Saul to visit him, for he wanted to hear the word of God. But Elymas, the sorcerer (as his name means in Greek), interfered and urged the governor to pay no attention to what Barnabas and Saul said. He was trying to keep the governor from believing. Saul, also known as Paul, was filled with the Holy Spirit, and he looked the sorcerer in the eye. Then he said, "You son of the devil, full of every sort of deceit and fraud, and enemy of all that is good! Will you never stop perverting the true ways of the Lord? Watch now, for the Lord has laid his hand of punishment upon you, and you will be struck blind. You will not see the sunlight for some time." Instantly mist and darkness came over the man's eyes, and he began groping around begging for someone to take his hand and lead him. When the governor saw what had happened, he became a believer, for he was astonished at the teaching about the Lord.
>
> — ACTS 13:6-12

In Acts 13:10, Paul looked the sorcerer in the eye and said, *"You son of the Devil."* Jesus taught that not everyone is a sheep. There are sheep, there are wolves, and there are wolves in sheep's clothing, and you should act accordingly.

The governor was won over to the Lord because he saw that Paul carried power over the demonic opposition against him. Life doesn't always work according to your human understanding. The wicked think their deceitful schemes can cause people to turn against the Lord, but when Paul took authority over the sorcerer, he had to move out of the way. The demons sitting on the souls nearby were removed, and the men became believers. Life is not physical; life is spiritual.

> But there was a certain man named Ananias who, with his wife, Sapphira, sold some property. He brought part of the money to the apostles, claiming it was the full amount. With his wife's consent, he kept the rest. Then Peter said, "Ananias, why have you let Satan fill your heart? You lied to the Holy Spirit, and you kept some of the money for yourself. The property was yours to sell or not sell, as you wished. And after selling it, the money was also yours to give away. How could you do a thing like this? You weren't lying to us but to God!" As soon as Ananias heard these words, he fell to the floor and died. Everyone who heard about it was terrified. Then some young men got up, wrapped him in a sheet, and took him out and buried him. About three hours later his wife came in, not knowing what had happened. Peter asked her, "Was this the price you and your husband received for your land?" "Yes," she replied, "that was the price." And Peter said, "How could the two of you even think of conspiring to test the Spirit of the Lord like this? The young men who buried your husband are just outside the door, and they will carry you out, too." Instantly, she fell to the floor and died. When the young men came in and saw that she was dead, they carried her out and buried her beside her husband. Great fear gripped the entire church and everyone else who heard what had happened.
>
> — ACTS 5:1-11

After reading the Book of Acts, you might have to admit that you have an American Gospel, not the real Gospel. If Acts chapter 5 were to happen today, every blogger would blast Peter, claiming he wasn't acting in love. But Peter didn't kill anyone; God was the One who struck Ananias dead. Was He not acting in love?

A policeman doesn't shoot an armed robber holding hostages at a 7-Eleven out of hate; he does it out of love for innocent people. When someone devotes their life to destroying innocent people, they are an enemy of the Gospel of Jesus Christ. This is clear in both the Old and

New Testaments. They fall into a specific category called wicked people. The Lord is angry with the wicked every day, along with everyone who doesn't share His anger. The Bible instructs us to love what is good and hate what is evil.

God's response to Ananias and Sapphira's deceit wasn't in vain; it helped grow the Early Church.

> The apostles were performing many miraculous signs and wonders among the people. And all the believers were meeting regularly at the Temple in the area known as Solomon's Colonnade. But no one else dared to join them, even though all the people had high regard for them. Yet more and more people believed and were brought to the Lord—crowds of both men and women.
> — ACTS 5:12-14

Oftentimes, people receive immediate deliverance in my meetings. It's not because I have superior ministerial skills; it's because I love them with all my heart, and I have an equal hatred for the thing destroying them. We're not anointed to pray for deliverance; we're anointed to preach deliverance under the inspiration of the Holy Ghost. There is a doctrine that overthrows opposition. When I pray a rebuke, it carries a weight.

God never said The Church would multiply by the slaughtering of its saints. That's not in the Bible. Some saints in the Catholic Church believe that, but there's zero scriptural evidence to support that claim. The seed for the multiplication of The Church is the preaching of the Gospel of Jesus Christ, which you can't do if you're dead. I don't teach a doctrine for all Christians to be murdered. Believers should live, prosper, and declare that Jesus is alive so others will be saved.

We all know of missionaries who died overseas, but what about missionaries with stories of radical intervention from God that saved their lives? Is He spinning lottery balls in Heaven to see which five missionaries He will save each year while the rest are killed? Those who claim, "How many of you know we could die at any time?" usually die early. The Bible says, *"Death and life are in the power of the tongue"* (Proverbs 18:21). It also says, *"A man will be satisfied by the fruit of his lips"* (Proverbs 18:20).

While some people are busy cursing themselves with their own tongue, others get a revelation and speak, *"No weapon formed against me will prosper. Every tongue that rises up against me, I will cast down"* (Isaiah 54:17). Those with revelation hear corrupt authority threaten death if they don't close their churches down, and they reply, "If you are alive tomorrow morning, I'll quit the ministry." Then watch as the person opposing them dies, and they continue in the power of God. When the Devil challenges you, open your mouth and fire back. My goal in writing this book is to place the Word of God in your spirit so you'll have something in you to fire back when confronted.

If God wanted everyone to be martyrs, why do some die and some survive? How come some have a dramatic intervention? The hallmark verses from the Bible for a believer are found in Acts 10:34-35, *"God is no respecter of persons, but in every nation, he accepts those who fear him and do what is right."* God doesn't have favorites. God doesn't pick random people to spare. There are people who, when confronted, lay down and take whatever life gives them, and there are those who understand the authority that's been given to them to fight back and win.

If someone tried to break into our church and steal our equipment, and we found them dead, I would not shed a single tear. I would know the Lord is watching over the camp of the righteous. That's the God I serve. I serve Jehovah, the Mighty Man of War. I serve the God of the Bible and the Jesus contained in Scripture, the Prince of Peace, the King of kings, with eyes like flames of fire, with a two-edged sword that proceeds out of His mouth.

When God appeared before Saul on the road to Damascus, Saul fell as if dead, and so did the men with him. They thought they were listening to thunder when He spoke. Jesus personally stopped Paul's persecution, which means someone was praying. Every action God takes requires the hand of God and man working in partnership. I have a hedge of protection, and it's in full effect.

> I have found my servant David. I have anointed him with my
> holy oil. I will steady him with my hand; with my powerful
> arm I will make him strong. His enemies will not defeat him,
> nor will the wicked overpower him. I will beat down his
> adversaries before him and destroy those who hate him. My
> faithfulness and unfailing love will be with him, and by my
> authority he will grow in power.
>
> — PSALM 89:20-24

God promised to beat down your foes and plague those who hate you. God is a God of vengeance. Some might say, "Vengeance is mine," but God said it belongs to Him. You can call Him to invoke vengeance. We don't kill people; God is our killer.

I could recount stories from now until Jesus comes of how God avenged the enemies of His servants. Most of them would be from overseas because they operate in that mentality by necessity.

There's a reason we started with twenty-five pastors in Asbury Park and ended with three as twenty-two backed out. When protesters emerged, pastors became afraid. In North America, The Church rarely knows how to deal with demonic opposition. They usually wait for it to disappear. But you have to attack it with the sword of the Spirit. God still knows how to avenge His elect.

> Those who live in the shelter of the Most High will find rest in
> the shadow of the Almighty. This I declare about the Lord:
> He alone is my refuge, my place of safety; he is my God, and
> I trust him. For he will rescue you from every trap and
> protect you from deadly disease. He will cover you with his
> feathers. He will shelter you with his wings. His faithful
> promises are your armor and protection. Do not be afraid of
> the terrors of the night, nor the arrow that flies in the day.
> Do not dread the disease that stalks in darkness, nor the
> disaster that strikes at midday. Though a thousand fall at
> your side, though ten thousand are dying around you, these

> evils will not touch you. Just open your eyes, and see how the wicked are punished. If you make the Lord your refuge, if you make the Most High your shelter, no evil will conquer you; no plague will come near your home.
>
> — PSALM 91:1-10

The Devil is not allowed to attack us with sickness. He's not even allowed anywhere near us. My life is hidden, and so is yours. I don't make any allowances for the Devil to attack my wife, child, car, equipment, or anything that belongs to me. No attack of the Devil will come near your home. That's what the Word of God declares.

> For he will order his angels to protect you wherever you go. They will hold you up with their hands so you won't even hurt your foot on a stone. You will trample upon lions and cobras; you will crush fierce lions and serpents under your feet! The Lord says, "I will rescue those who love me. I will protect those who trust in my name. When they call on me, I will answer; I will be with them in trouble. I will rescue and honor them. I will reward them with a long life and give them my salvation.
>
> — PSALM 91:11-16

> When the seventy-two disciples returned, they joyfully reported to him, "Lord, even the demons obey us when we use your name!" "Yes," he told them, "I saw Satan fall from heaven like lightning! Look, I have given you authority over all the power of the enemy, and you can walk among snakes and scorpions and crush them. Nothing will injure you."
>
> — LUKE 10:17-19

Jesus said in the New Testament, *"I have given you authority over all the power of the enemy"* (Luke 10:19). Does death come from the power of the enemy? Premature death surely does. Persecution against The Church or threats against your life for preaching the Gospel are from the Devil. God gave you authority over these things. You don't have to wait for anything linked to demonic power to disappear. You can destroy them with the power of God.

The second half of Luke 10:19 says, *"You can walk amongst snakes and scorpions and crush them. Nothing will injure you."* I will crush the Devil under my feet. That's the power Jesus gave us. Then He finished with, *"And nothing shall by any means harm you."* Nothing about this verse is confusing. I can't understand how so many preachers mess it up. I don't make an allowance for injury because I preach the Gospel. Some would counter, "Well, the Bible teaches, turn the other cheek," but if you apply what I am teaching you, nothing will make it to either of your cheeks. We don't have to fight. We speak and God fights for us.

Christians who don't understand how to read and study the Bible ask why the Bible tells storys of believers being beaten in jail, or of Paul leaving Miletus sick at Troas.

Understand this about the Bible: It is not the Quran. It doesn't turn every character into a superhero. It informs you that David committed adultery. It tells when Elijah was so depressed he wanted to die. It describes how Samson goofed up his life, and recounts when people couldn't be healed.

If I were to give an account of my ministry, I'd tell you that not everyone I've prayed for received healing. That doesn't negate what the Bible teaches about healing. The Bible tells you the whole truth. When Paul prayed for Miletus and had to leave him sick at Troas, that's what happened. They didn't get what the Bible said, but that doesn't mean you can't have it. The Bible simply states what happened. It tells the truth. It also tells you that when Peter's shadow fell across people, they were healed. The Bible is honest.

Paul was put in prison. He was also out of prison within two hours, then he started a church, and then he died. Paul knew everything would happen the way it did. Paul didn't abruptly drop dead. He didn't die until he proclaimed, *"I have fought a good fight. I have finished the race"* (2 Timothy 4:7). I don't follow Paul; I follow Jesus. I'm looking unto Jesus, the Author and Finisher of our faith. Your faith and expectations should be in Jesus.

When they came to arrest Jesus, He said, *"I am He,"* and his enemies all fell backward. He said, *"Don't you realize that I could ask my Father for thousands of angels to protect us, and he would send them instantly?"* (Matthew 26:53). He could have blown Pilate out the back wall. When Pilot asked Jesus, *"Are you going to remain silent? Don't you realize I have the power to take your life or set you free?"* Jesus replied, *"You have no power over Me whatsoever, except what's been given to you by the Father. Nobody takes My life. I lay it down willingly"* (John 19:11;10:18). When they tried to kill Jesus before His time, He walked through the crowd, and no one dared to lay a hand on Him.

Jesus is our example, and no one could touch Jesus until He laid down His life. I believe Paul laid down his life, it wasn't taken from him. When they tried to stone him to death, he popped up, went back into the city, and continued to preach. Don't make any allowance in your spirit for so-called "persecution."

PART II
YOUR DEFENSE STRATEGY

CHAPTER 6

LIVE HOLY

SANCTIFICATION SECURES VICTORY

God promised total victory. He never said there wouldn't be *attempts* to destroy you, but defeat is not associated with serving God. He specifically said that defeat is part of the curse for not fully serving Him, but when you fully serve the Lord, victory belongs to you.

> Oh, the joys of those who do not follow the advice of the wicked, or stand around with sinners, or join in with mockers. But they delight in the law of the Lord, meditating on it day and night. They are like trees planted along the riverbank, bearing fruit each season. Their leaves never wither, and they prosper in all they do.
>
> — PSALM 1:1-3

Three blessings come to those who serve Him and live holy:

1. They bear fruit in every season.
2. Their leaves never wither.
3. They prosper in all they do.

Many people say things like, "I'm in a dry season." I don't know who convinced them of this. There are no dry seasons for the children of God. God promised He wouldn't allow anything to wither your leaves or keep you from bearing fruit. Everything you do is blessed.

God promised you a long, fruitful life. He will give you a plan to remain fruitful and victorious all year. Our God is a God of acceleration. Just like Psalm 23:6 says, *"Surely goodness and mercy will follow me all the days of my life."*

When the national military mobilized to kill David, no one could get near him. Saul's bodyguards were all fast asleep as David cut off a piece of his garment. God put them to sleep, and no one woke up. He protected David (1 Samuel 24). But when David sinned, he didn't need to be attacked. The attack was magnetically drawn to him because of his sin. It's a clear illustration of the difference between holy and unholy living. Living holy brings you under God's hand of protection and favor, but sin causes you to step outside of God's protection. Proverbs 13:21 says, *"Trouble chases sinners; blessings chase the righteous."*

God told you that if you do what He tells you to do, He'll not only put you on top, He'll also keep you on top. From the time Samuel anointed David, he never went backward. He went from living in his father's home to working in the king's palace, and by the end of the next chapter, he had killed Goliath.

David's only hiccup came when he stopped doing what God called him to do and his child died as a result. In the season when kings went to war, David stayed home, became comfortable, saw a lady taking a bath and committed adultery. That sin opened the door to destruction. But when you live a holy life, you'll be amazed at how little spiritual warfare you must engage in.

Living a holy life and keeping the commands of God isn't just about not sinning. We don't stop there. It's also about actively pursuing what God's called you to do. Living holy slams the door on the Devil's ability to touch you.

> "But if you refuse to listen to the Lord your God and do not obey all the commands and decrees I am giving you today, all these curses will come and overwhelm you: Your towns and your fields will be cursed. Your fruit baskets and breadboards will be cursed. Your children and your crops will be cursed. The offspring of your herds and flocks will be cursed. Wherever you go and whatever you do, you will be cursed. The Lord himself will send on you curses, confusion, and frustration in everything you do, until at last you are completely destroyed for doing evil and abandoning me."
>
> — DEUTERONOMY 28:15-20

A friend and former felon recently received salvation. Before he was saved, I heard him say, "Man, my sister's boyfriend broke into my house and stole my gun and sold it in downtown Pittsburgh for crack. Now I have a gun with my prints on it floating around downtown. If someone commits a crime with it, I'll go to jail for life."

My friend made every effort to clean up his life, but a robber broke into his house and stole his gun. *Trouble chases sinners.* Many of you are familiar with how that works, but I want you to understand that blessings will find their way to you when you serve the Lord with all your heart, all your soul, and all your physical strength. Without trying, blessings will track you down.

Many Christians prefer to believe a hard life comes with serving God and quote the scripture that says, "*A righteous man, though he falls seven times, gets back up.* That's a great scripture to preach to felons in prison. It's a great scripture to preach to a Christian who backslides—you can get back up, but you don't use that verse as scriptural grounds for failure or sin. "Well, I know I'm going to fall seven times this year. I don't know when or why. Maybe it'll be adultery. Maybe it'll be alcoholism. Who knows, maybe I'll murder someone, but I know God will give me power." That's a pretty stupid outlook on life.

A songwriter wrote a song called *Keep Me in Your Reach*. I remember listening to it and thinking how stupid it was. The verses went: "Sometimes I do things my own way. Sometimes I go out on my own, but Father, please keep me in your reach." The songwriter is a guy I like, but he was essentially singing about how his goal in life was to do things the way he wanted while asking God to not allow him to get too far out of His reach.

One of the reasons for my preaching style and content is that I've seen what stupid doctrines produce. Jesus said, *"You will know them by their fruits"* (Matthew 7:16). I watched that "Lord-keep-me-in-your-reach" guy. It turns out he bought gifts for women he wasn't married to with church money, bankrupted his personal and ministry accounts, and lost everything, including his marriage. He held a stupid viewpoint on life, and he suffered the consequences. Don't live like that.

Make this your prayer: "Father, as I prize the wisdom of Your Word, thank You for causing me to walk on straight paths as You promised in Proverbs 4:11. Thank You that as I walk, nothing will hold me back and when I run, I'll never stumble."

Dr. Billy Graham went home to be with the Lord in 2018. His life exemplifies this sentiment. He didn't have any hiccups. When the Lord opened the door of favor to him in his thirties, it was straight up from there. You can have that same favor. God doesn't have favorites. God just has people who quit and die and people who stick with it and live a victorious life.

Everything continued to grow for Billy Graham. When he was ninety years old, he told his son Franklin he wanted to do one final crusade. Since he didn't have the strength to do it in a stadium, he spoke to the entire world from his home in the mountains of North Carolina. His message, titled *Are You Ready to Die*, was heard and seen around the world and is still being seen today, years after his homegoing. He never had to take an offering for the event. It was all paid in advance. At the ripe age of ninety, he did the greatest work for God he had ever done. He concluded a life of service in ministry by preaching to an estimated 2.2 billion people around the world and counting. He stayed with his wife, Ruth, until she went to Heaven. Now they're back together again. His son is serving the Lord, and his daughter, Anne, is a great preacher. Pick your examples wisely. Be followers of those who obtain the promise of God by faith and patience (Hebrews 6:12).

There are certain conferences I will never preach and ministers I will never associate with, because they're on wife number two or three, or they drink. I don't want any part of that lifestyle. I don't care if they're great preachers or have miracles. I don't want to have a greater degree of miracles in my ministry at the expense of losing my wife and missing Heaven.

Ministers with children who serve the Lord don't tell them, "Daddy is tired from preaching. Go play in another room." You don't give your best to the people and your worst to your family. Give your best to the people, then let God refill the wind in your sails and give even better to your family. You don't have to sacrifice anything.

I follow people who live holy because I want what they have to rub off on me. I follow men who treat their wives right. Preachers shouldn't speak to their wives in the same tone they use to speak to the Devil. I have friendships with people in fifty-year marriages, and it's taught me the proper tone to use toward my wife, how to touch my wife, and how to treat my children.

THREE VOWS EVERY CHRISTIAN SHOULD MAKE

These are the three practical vows that produce practical victory.

1. I will make it to Heaven.

Vow to do everything necessary to make Heaven. Refuse to backslide or give in to sin. Choose to live holy. You will receive an overcomer's crown when you get to Heaven, just like Jesus said. *"All who are victorious will wear my crown, and I will cause them to sit on my throne"* (Revelation 3:21).

> "Write this letter to the angel of the church in Laodicea. This is the message from the one who is the Amen—the faithful and true witness, the beginning of God's new creation: I know all the things you do, that you are neither hot nor cold. I wish that you were one or the other!"
>
> — REVELATION 3:14-15

This passage of Scripture wasn't written to the sinners of Laodicea; it was written to the *church* of Laodicea. People who claim that salvation relieves you from all worry must also believe Jesus had a poor revelation of the Bible. He returned from Heaven and instructed John to write seven letters to seven churches. Of those seven letters, six were warnings essentially warning the church to get their act together, or they're going to Hell. These are words written to churches and pastors.

> "I know all the things you do, that you are neither hot nor cold. I wish that you were one or the other! But since you are like lukewarm water, neither hot nor cold, I will spit you out of my mouth! You say, 'I am rich. I have everything I want. I don't need a thing!' And you don't realize that you are wretched and miserable and poor and blind and naked. So I advise you to buy gold from me—gold that has been purified by fire. Then you will be rich. Also buy white garments from me so you will not be shamed by your nakedness, and ointment for your eyes so you will be able to see. I correct and discipline everyone I love. So be diligent and turn from your indifference."
>
> — REVELATION 3:15-19

The chief reason people will end up in Hell is indifference. There will be murderers in Hell, but far more people will find themselves there due to their own apathy. A tiny percentage of people have a firm opinion against God; most are just indifferent—they have no passion. Jesus warned the end-time church to be diligent and turn from indifference. There will be many surprised people in Hell. Someone will have to explain to them where they are and how they got there, but no one will be in Heaven by accident.

Everyone who makes Heaven will make it because of a definitive decision to turn from sin, receive Jesus Christ, and live every day in forward motion. I am more on fire for God today than I was yesterday, and I'll be more on fire for God tomorrow than I am today. That doesn't just happen. That's the result of a decision to get rid of sin, keep it away, and engage God in the way He instructed. Pray always in the Holy Ghost, building up your most precious faith (Ephesians 6:18). The Word of God builds you, so stay in it.

> "I correct and discipline everyone I love. So be diligent and turn from your indifference. Look! I stand at the door and knock. If you hear my voice and open the door, I will come in, and we will share a meal together as friends. Those who are victorious will sit with me on my throne."
>
> — REVELATION 3:19-21

I don't teach on victory for fun. You need a spirit of victory to make it to Heaven. I refuse to be discouraged or offended because I have victory. The Lord gave David victory wherever he went, and that's His plan for you too. Carrying a spirit of victory is the difference between going to Heaven and going to Hell. When you refuse to quit or be defeated, He that began a good work in you shall bring it to completion. The Devil has no chance. He can't determine anything. He's voted against you, but God has voted for you. Everything else is up to you. Satan is under your feet; he can't be blamed for anything. Forget demons, they're lower than Satan, and witches are lower still. You're seated with Christ in heavenly places, and you carry victory in your spirit.

> "Look! I stand at the door and knock. If you hear my voice and open the door, I will come in, and we will share a meal together as friends. Those who are victorious will sit with me on my throne, just as I was victorious and sat with my Father on his throne. Anyone with ears to hear must listen to the Spirit and understand what he is saying to the churches."
>
> — REVELATION 3:20-22

Victory is not automatic; you must pursue it. The default is Hell. The default is divorce. The default is children who don't serve the Lord. The default is sickness and disease. The default is poverty. The default is failure. You don't have to do anything to receive those outcomes, but if you're going to obtain what God promised, you must pursue it, overtake it, and grab it by faith. The faith I'm referring to isn't for survival or comfort during the storm—it's a faith that takes ground for the Kingdom of God. That faith is being imparted to you today, in Jesus' name.

2. I will not divorce my spouse.

Refuse to divorce your spouse. This is a decision within your control, especially for husbands. Any failure in the home is the man's fault. The man is the high priest of the home. Eve may have done all the talking with the Devil and screwed everything up, but God held Adam accountable. A man oversees his home. I will give an account, not only for whether I make Heaven but for what happens with Adalis and Camila. You're responsible for what God has given you. When God puts you in charge, He provides the power to succeed along with it. You must be personally accountable. You can't be like Adam in his sinful state and attempt to pass the buck. Take control of your home.

If the Pittsburgh Steelers have a bad year in the NFL, they don't fire all seventy players; they fire the coach. Whomever God puts in charge is the one who gives an account, but to whomever God makes the head, He gives the power to carry out the task.

Most divorced people are also against divorce. It's the source of much pain. Decide today that you will have what God said belongs to you. He said, *"What God has joined together, let not man separate"* (Matthew 19:6). You can have a successful marriage, and you should vow to work through whatever problems arise so that your marriage develops into what God has ordained it to be.

God gave you a wife. He didn't say, "He who finds a wife, finds a ball and chain." He said, *"He who finds a wife, finds a good thing and obtaineth favor from the Lord"* (Proverbs 18:22). I know who I was before I married Adalis, and I know who I am now. I've never had to drag her around in the ministry. She's been a jet engine. For every book I've written, she's written two. She's the best. That's why God created marriage—to give you someone you enjoy coming home to.

The Devil wants to destroy your marriage because he knows you can't succeed in a nest full of thorns. Birds don't make nests out of thorn branches. You need peace in your home. That's why the Devil attacks it, but God gave you the power to drive the enemy out and have a blessed marriage that gives you strength, in Jesus' name.

3. My children will serve the Lord.

> I know him, that he will command his children and his household after him, and they shall keep the way of the Lord, to do justice and judgment; that the Lord may bring upon Abraham that which he hath spoken of him.
>
> — GENESIS 18:19 (KJV)

God chose Abraham because he had command over his household. God trusted him to command, not suggest, that all those under him keep the way of the Lord. When God told Abraham to circumcise himself, Abraham ensured all 318 men who lived in his home did so, too. Abraham carried the authority to command his children, their households, and anyone under his authority to keep the way of the Lord. I've witnessed that in my own family, so I believe it.

Joshua said, *"As for me and my house, we will serve the* Lord*"* (Joshua 24:15). You can carry authority for your house. You can choose to have the exact opposite of what you see in the world.

> Lo, children are a heritage of the Lord: and the fruit of the womb is his reward. As arrows are in the hand of a mighty man; so are children of the youth. Happy is the man that hath his quiver full of them: they shall not be ashamed, but they shall speak with the enemies in the gate.
>
> — PSALM 127:3-5 (KJV)

> "I have singled him out so that he will direct his sons and their families to keep the way of the Lord by doing what is right and just. Then I will do for Abraham all that I have promised."
>
> — GENESIS 18:19

You have the authority to bring your entire household under subjection and into covenant with God. The Bible says, *"Train up a child in the way they should go, and when they grow old, they will not depart from it"* (Proverbs 22:6).

I don't run around hosting crusades and preaching revival meetings to see other people's children saved while mine goes to Hell. It's not happening. I will not have the Lord use me to restore people's homes and then come home and lose my wife. I wreck the Devil's hold on other people's homes, kick him out of my household, and keep him out for good. That's total victory.

Real victory entails going to Heaven, having a marriage that God intended, and having children who aren't trouble for you. Your children won't be a source of tears; your children will be a source of laughter.

> And the Lord gave them rest, round about from all their trouble.
>
> — JOSHUA 21:44 (KJV)

> The blessing of the Lord makes a person rich, and he adds no sorrow with it.
>
> — PROVERBS 10:22

When you serve God, He will permanently eject sorrow from your life.

> The joy of the Lord becomes your strength. Happy are the people whose God is the Lord. The Lord shall increase you more and more, you and your children.
>
> — PSALM 115:14

> Praise ye the Lord. Blessed is the man that feareth the Lord, that delighteth greatly in His commandments. His seed shall be mighty upon earth: the generation of the upright shall be blessed.
>
> — PSALM 112:1-2 (KJV)

Victory in marriage, victory with your children, and victory within your household are present all throughout the Bible. When they laid the Ark of the Covenant in Obed Edom's house, word got back to David that his sheep and cows were multiplying and everything he owned was blessed. David decided to reclaim the Ark after hearing how blessed Obed Edom's house had become because he valued the blessing of God. The blessing of God is the answer to the struggles of man. God's blessing erases struggle. It causes you to prevail, increase, and overflow.

> Thou anointest my head with oil; my cup runneth over. Surely goodness and mercy will follow me all the days of my life: and I will dwell in the house of the Lord for ever.
>
> — PSALM 23:5-6 (KJV)

> When the Lord brought back his exiles to Jerusalem, it was like a dream! We were filled with laughter, and we sang for joy.
>
> — PSALM 126:1-2

When God brought Israel out of captivity, they began to laugh and sing, not cry. God is a God of joy. The joy of the Lord is our strength—not the tears of Heaven. God is not a sad lady on an organ in a Catholic church. God is happy. *"Happy are the people whose God is the Lord"* (Psalm 144:15).

> We were filled with laughter, and we sang for joy. And the other nations said, "What amazing things the Lord has done for them." Yes, the Lord has done amazing things for us! What joy! Restore our fortunes, Lord, as streams renew the desert. Those who plant in tears will harvest with shouts of joy. They weep as they go to plant their seed, but they sing as they return with the harvest.
>
> — PSALM 126:2-6

> Unless the Lord builds a house, the work of the builders is wasted. Unless the Lord protects a city, guarding it with sentries will do no good. It is useless for you to work so hard from early morning until late at night, anxiously working for food to eat; for God gives rest to his loved ones.
>
> — PSALM 127:1-2

If you live a holy life and do what God tells you to do, you'll be amazed by how little spiritual warfare you must engage in. Life is not fighting all the time. God gave them rest, roundabout from all their enemies.

You may be like David and have to be the first in your family to defeat and break barriers. But once David cleared out all the enemies, Solomon enjoyed peace throughout his entire lifetime. Someone must be the first to break poverty, sickness, fighting, alcoholism, or drug addiction. But once you win that battle in the spirit, your children will enjoy rest and peace throughout their lifetime. Make up your mind today that as for me and my house, we will serve the Lord!

CHAPTER 7

BE SPIRIT-LED

> They are like trees planted along the riverbank, bearing fruit each season. Their leaves never wither, and they prosper in all they do.
>
> — PSALM 1:3

The Lord spoke to my spirit a while ago and said, "Jonathan, why don't you make plans like you actually believe that verse, that I will cause anything you're involved in to prosper?"

The Bible tells us to *"Listen to what I say and you will have a long, good life"* (Proverbs 4:10). Some people think it's a misrepresentation of the Gospel to teach that your life will get better if you follow God and His Word. But the Bible is the wisdom of God in print, and it carries the power of God to follow that wisdom. It doesn't say, "If you follow the wisdom of God, who knows where it will take you?" God told you the destination, but when you don't know your destination, any place looks like a possibility.

God took the time to show Abraham a picture of his destination. *"Look up into the sky and count the stars if you can. That's how many descendants you will have!"* (Genesis 15:5). Abraham knew where he was going, then called those things that were not as though they were when he changed his name from Abram to Abraham, meaning exalted father. When Abraham introduced himself as "the father of many nations," he wasn't just saying it. He was certain of what God had shown him. He knew he would have children as numerous as the sand on the seashore. Think about that. The promise of Abraham is not just for the 7.5 million Jewish people.

> And now that you belong to Christ, you are the true children of Abraham. You are his heirs, and God's promise to Abraham belongs to you.
>
> — GALATIANS 3:29

The Bible says the real seed of Abraham is all who put their faith in Jesus Christ—that's upward of one billion people. Abraham's seed turned out to be as numerous as the sand, just like God said.

God will always fulfill His promise, but you must have a picture of where you're headed. If the biggest church you've ever seen has seven hundred people, when you reach five hundred members, you'll think you're knocking it out of the park. But when you visit a church with three million people in attendance, you'll realize you have a long way to go.

Study God's Word and get a picture of where God wants you to be. He doesn't want you broke and struggling. God doesn't want you to save up for a vacation. God wants to give you the resort property that all the heathen people save up to afford. The owner, not the borrower. The head, not the tail.

Prosperity isn't owning a Mercedes; prosperity is owning a Mercedes dealership. That's where God wants to take you. God has a throne for you on this Earth, if you're interested. Ask Abraham and Isaac. He said, *"I will bless you and make you famous. I will make your name great"* (Genesis 12:2).

God said, *"My child, listen to me and do as I say."* He didn't tell you to believe what He said—*"Do* what I say." Doing proves your belief. Faith acts on what the Word of God says. "Do what I say, and you'll have a long, good life. I will teach you wisdom's ways and lead you in straight paths. When you walk, you won't be held back. When you run, you won't stumble" (Proverbs 4:10-12).

God promised to teach you wisdom's ways and lead you in straight paths when you obey His commands. Walking in straight paths means you won't bounce all over the place. You won't be a preacher for ten years, a car salesman for five years, then a life coach for seven years.

Billy Graham did one thing—win souls. I don't know if he ever prayed for one sick person. That wasn't his ministry. When the Healing Movement hit, he never attempted to join them—neither was he against them. He invited Oral Roberts to his meetings to pray for the sick. He loved the men of God in the healing movement, but he knew his job was to win souls, and he stuck with it.

You can walk straight paths, and God will give you the power to stay on the path. No more detours in your life, no more going left and right. No more going up and down.

> When you walk, you won't be held back; when you run, you won't stumble. Take hold of my instructions; don't let them go. Guard them, for they are the key to life. Don't do as the wicked do, and don't follow the path of evildoers. Don't even think about it; don't go that way. Turn away and keep moving. For evil people can't sleep until they've done their evil deed for the day. They can't rest until they've caused someone to stumble. They eat the food of wickedness and drink the wine of violence! But the path of the righteous is like the first gleam of dawn, which shines ever brighter until the full light of day.
>
> — PROVERBS 4:12-18

The last time I was in Arizona, I woke up just before sunrise because of the time difference. Adalis and Camilla were still sleeping, so I went out to the porch. I watched as the sun peeked over the horizon, and the morning light grew brighter and brighter as it broke over the desert. I stared as the skies went from midnight blue to a bright, vibrant blue.

In Arizona, by the time the sun rises about three-quarters of the way in the sky, you can fry an egg in the palm of your hand. I sat there watching with a cold drink, and a scripture came to mind: *"The path of the righteous is like the morning sun, shining ever brighter till the full light of day"* (Proverbs 4:18). I noticed the sun didn't zigzag. It wasn't attacked by darkness for an hour. In Arizona, there haven't been clouds since before 500 AD. It's cloudless as the sun rises, and it never quits rising or stops getting brighter.

The Bible says that those who take hold of His instruction will shine brighter and brighter until the full light of day. In the same way, nothing can stop the sun from rising, nothing can stop you from succeeding. The sun doesn't become depressed halfway up and retreat. The sun doesn't battle demons that keep it from shining brighter. When you run, nothing will hold you back, just like nothing can stop the sun from rising.

People have been duped into believing life is full of ups and downs—mountains and valleys, but when you stick with God, He gives you an upward trajectory that nothing can stop.

CHAPTER 8

RESIST

It's normal to be challenged; it's unscriptural to be defeated. When David fled to a cave, six hundred men followed and quickly joined with him to become his army. They became his personal force, along with thirty mighty men who fought beside him.

Almost all of David's Psalms begin with his back against the wall: "I'm in despair. I don't know what to do." Then it changes halfway through the Psalm. It never ends depressingly. "Yet my hope is in the Lord who made heaven." Then by the end, he snaps out of it, takes what the Devil meant for bad, and flips it for good.

Paul is another example of this. Paul wasn't depressed when he was in prison. When they threw him in jail, he started singing. Not only did he break out of prison, he led the jailer to the Lord. He was in jail for about two hours. One minute he was locked up and the next he was living it up in the jailer's jacuzzi and staying in his Roman government home. Bible scholars believe the jailer later became the pastor of the church in Philippi.

When Paul was shipwrecked on the island of Malta he not only lost all possessions, he didn't even have freedom. His clothes were soaked and unusable—that's poverty, but within 72 hours, he was in his own home. The Bible says the entire island showered him with high-honor gifts.

Could you call those 72 hours a valley? Maybe, but if you view it in the context of a week, the experience appears more like a mountain. When everyone in an entire town brings you money on Friday, it doesn't really matter what happens on Monday and Tuesday.

There's an old preacher who said, "One day of favor will erase the memories of a thousand days of labor." It's a matter of perspective. A 72-hour challenge, ending with the greatest victory you've ever had, sounds to me like your enemy coming from one direction but God making them run in seven. The Bible is full of these kinds of situations. I don't view them as valleys.

If the Bible said that Paul was put in prison for seventeen years, and in the seventeenth year, Paul sang praises unto God and was released from prison, you might conclude that sometimes there's a valley season in life, but that's not Paul's story. He was in prison for a few hours, released, shipwrecked in Malta, and within one chapter, he was living in his own home—that's not a season of life. We'll dive deeper into the life of Paul later in this book.

Will there be challenges? Will confrontations come? Sure. Will the Devil try to attack you? Yes, but you must remain joyful and maintain a victorious mentality. I don't believe in valleys or mountains. I believe we're seated with Christ; that's what the Bible teaches. There are no verses in the Bible about you being a mountain. The Bible says God will make you the head and never the tail, on top, never at the bottom. You're seated with Christ in heavenly places, far above (Ephesians 2:6).

There are no ups and downs with Jesus in the gospels. There were two failed attacks on His life. The first time, they tried to push Him over a cliff to no avail. The second time, they picked up stones to kill Him and He walked through the crowd, and no one dared lay a hand on Him. Jesus suffered a voluntary and momentary challenge when he laid down His life, and within three days, He rose from the dead for the salvation of the world. That's victory!

When the soldiers arrived to arrest Jesus, He asked, "Who are you looking for?" He knew what would happen, but He still approached them. He could have escaped, but He chose to lay down His life.

"We're looking for Jesus of Nazareth," the soldiers responded.

As soon as Jesus replied, "I am He," they all fell backward to the ground. He could have left the scene and evaded arrest, but He was quiet and gave Himself up.

When He was brought before Pilate, He remained quiet. He didn't utter a word until Pilate wrongfully claimed he had the power to crucify Him.

Jesus could have called twelve legions of angels and wiped the floor with the whole city. *"Jesus answered, 'You could have no power at all against Me unless it had been given you from above. Therefore, the one who delivered Me to you has the greater sin'"* (John 19:11).

God wants to be glorified in your death, and there's nothing glorious about death caused by sickness or disease. Paul foretold his last assignment and death. God chooses the time. I can't be randomly shot, stabbed, diseased, or die apart from His choosing unless I fall into sin.

When believers are faced with difficult situations, it's not a valley, it's a challenge. God will quickly show you how to overcome the challenge and come out the other side with more than if the challenge never came. When trouble comes, God not only gives you an anointing to defeat it, He also provides a plan to flip it and emerge with a glorious testimony.

There are limitations on what the enemy can do. Don't ever concede sickness. Do not concede your health as an attack, as many preachers do. If I were a normal preacher, I'd say, "Well, as we're getting ready to do this crusade, I'm sure the enemy will try to make me sick." No, he's not allowed to make me sick. *"Thou has put a hedge of protection around him, his family, and everything he owns"* (Job 1:10). He's not allowed on my property.

The Devil can't attack you with what Christ has redeemed you from. You will have trials and tribulations in this world, but you must also be careful of what *you* allow. This is where Baptists and other denominations get it wrong. They think cancer is a trial or that Parkinson's disease is a test—it's not. James 5:14 says, *"Are any of you sick? You should call for the elders of the church to come and pray over you, anointing you with oil in the name of the Lord."* There's a different set of instructions for sickness than for problems.

 Never Mistake a Challenge for Defeat.

When American Pentecostal pastor and evangelist Lester Sumrall was preparing to start a church in China, the Chinese bank froze $2 million of the church's assets. The Chinese bank didn't want a church to be built. Lester Sumrall flew from Indiana to China and went to the bank's office to declare that if that money wasn't released, every member of the bank leadership would die, and their children would be filled with cancer. They turned the money loose in about two hours.

Similarly, Paul cursed the sorcerer with blindness when he tried to prevent the Gospel from being preached. There are things you pray *for*, and there are things you pray *against*.

When the apostles faced attacks in the Book of Acts, the Bible says, *"And through the hands of the apostles many signs and wonders were done among the people. And they were all with one accord in Solomon's Porch. Yet none of the rest dared join them, but the people esteemed them highly"* (Acts 5:12-13 NKJV). When the church loses the power to rebuke the forces of darkness, it encourages further attacks from the enemy. When you move to beat back the darkness, word gets out in Hell. You're going to be on one side or the other. You will either bust the Devil's head or get your head busted. You'll either be someone who demons run after or somebody who puts demons on the run. There's no in-between.

HOW TO PREVAIL IN EVERY BATTLE OF LIFE

> In the world you have tribulation and trials and distress and frustration; but be of good cheer [take courage; be confident, certain, undaunted]! For I have overcome the world. [I have deprived it of power to harm you and have conquered it for you.]
>
> — JOHN 16:33 (AMPC)

Challenges are normal and to be expected. Paul saw his situation as a challenge of imprisonment and knew he could defeat it with praise. Think of what might have happened had he just said, "Well, Barnabas, I thought we would have a longer ministry than this. The captain said they're not going to let us out. They may bring us to trial tomorrow and have us executed. Things don't always work out the way we planned. It's over."

Weeping may endure for one night. Anything longer than one night has overstayed the scriptural bounds of bringing tears to your life. *"Weeping may endure for a night, but joy comes in the morning"* (Psalm 30:5 **NKJV**).

Jesus never made concessions. When Jesus received word that Herod was upset by what He was preaching, He responded, "Go *tell that fox that I will keep on casting out demons and healing people today and tomorrow; and the third day I will accomplish my purpose"* (Luke 13:32). The Bible says in Isaiah 54:17, *"Every tongue that rises up against you, thou shalt condemn."* It doesn't say God will condemn every tongue; it says you will. *You* must speak. That same power and authority that Jesus and His disciples invoked still works today.

When I visited India, I met an evangelist who was confronted by military police at his five-star hotel after returning from preaching a crusade. They told him he was under arrest for saying things about Hindu gods that angered the people. He calmly stepped out of the car and replied, "That's fine. But know this: whichever police officer touches me first will go blind, his wife will die, and his children will fill with cancer." Every officer backed off, and he walked to his hotel room untouched. *"Every tongue that rises up against you, thou shalt condemn."*

HANDLING CRITICISM

Rodney Howard-Browne once said, "If you don't want criticism, then don't get out of bed in the morning. But then people will criticize you for not getting out of bed in the morning."

Verbal persecution is harmless. It doesn't do anything to you unless you let it. Ministers must lose the notion that doing everything right means everybody will like them. People hated Jesus. They demanded the release of a murderer in favor of the death of Jesus, and He did nothing wrong.

If I didn't understand how to disregard criticism, I would allow the opinions of others to shape what I post on social media. I post pictures of myself on our ministry jet to inspire other ministers, but not everyone finds them inspirational. If I allowed a couple of critical comments to affect me, it would deter me from posting similar photos in the future. But that's not how I operate because I know there's nothing I can do that won't elicit negative feedback from someone.

Suppose I was to hide all the pictures of the jet and never mention receiving it. It would probably take *Dateline* about ten months to discover and expose to everyone what I've hidden. That's why I make a point to openly show what I do. The same watch I wear when I'm not preaching, I wear while preaching. I'm not a guy who wears a Rolex around town and puts on a Casio to preach, so people think I need money. People can't expose things I've already revealed.

If you preach prosperity all the time, people who hate prosperity will leave. When I post photos of myself on a jet, there are no negative comments anymore because I ran those people off a long time ago. When you read the comments, seventy-five out of seventy-five are positive because I've preached it into people to believe Biblical prosperity.

You'll be criticized no matter what you do. There's no way to minister without receiving criticism. As soon as you settle that in your mind, you'll be much better off. Why let one negative person override seventy-four positive people? Why allow one devil to override fifty great people?

The Lord helped me understand this when I was preaching in Montreal. It was one of the first times we ever went on Facebook Live, and it was a great meeting. Some guy wrote three comments in big, lengthy paragraphs in all caps. "You're full of the Devil. What you're preaching is wrong. All you want is people's money. You talked about money for over thirty minutes tonight." It upset me. Not only did I get angry at him, but it affected my relationship with my wife—your wife notices, and so do your kids. I started to respond to him, and I felt the Lord speak to me. "You've allowed one idiot to wreck your view of what I did in that service. Sixty people were saved. Who cares if one guy didn't like what you said?" Then the Lord said, "If that bothers you, I will keep you at this level for your own sake. What will happen when you go on TV?"

If I hadn't learned to deal with criticism then, the 450 protesters who came later probably would have had me in the fetal position, sucking my thumb. But when heavier criticism came, God gave me the grace to handle it, and I didn't care.

When someone writes something nasty about me online, I just read it and move on. Everybody is welcome to their opinion. Insults are differences of opinion harshly expressed. I'm glad we have freedom of speech in this country. If people don't agree, they're free to disagree. They're also free to express their disagreement. It doesn't bother me. The guy who wrote that nasty comment in Montreal had zero followers. No one read what he wrote. Don't give people like him any space in your head.

Not only should you avoid responding to criticism, but you shouldn't let it affect you either. There are thousands of preachers who fast, pray, and win souls, but they have never gone to the next level in their ministry, because they're fragile. They're so sensitive in response to other's opinions that God keeps them small for their own sake. The higher you go, the greater the level of criticism. You must allow God to give you grace.

Benson Idahosa and Billy Graham's philosophy was: No attack, no defense. Don't attack anyone, and don't defend yourself against anyone either. Ahead of the Ashbury Park event, I was called a pedophile and other names on LGBTQ community message boards. I never responded. They're not my enemy. I want them to be saved. If I had responded on that message board, tensions would have flared when they realized they had my attention. You can't argue with someone who doesn't know you exist. But if you choose to engage, all the wolves will come out, and all the people without jobs will start arguing on social media.

Don't purposely post inflammatory things online. Christians do this too often. If I post or preach about healing, I do it to get sick people healed. It might also tick people off who don't believe in healing, but that's not my aim.

If I post a picture of me flying in a plane, it's not to tick off people, although some may choose to take offense. I post pictures like this to send a message to young people called into ministry who are being told it's hard and there's no money. I want to provide an example of how easy and fun it can be when it's done the right way. I do it to inspire people.

There was a time when it was considered wrong for a preacher to drive a car. Old Pentecostal manuscripts say things like, "I'm not one of these preachers with a $10,000 motor car." Preachers who drove Cadillacs in the fifties took a ton of heat. Now, it's normal for a preacher to have a nice car. I am willing to take the heat to normalize having a jet, so the next generation of evangelists can be home with their families.

When Kenneth Copeland taught about giving thousand-dollar seeds, people wanted to crucify him for it; now, it's normal. Brother Copeland and Brother Hagin took the heat. They moved the standard forward. Now, it's normal for church people to release Kingdom-sized seeds. I take the heat, so those who come after me have an easier and more fruitful run. Learn to handle the criticism that comes with doing great things for God and His Kingdom or be prepared to stay small.

CHAPTER 9

UNDERSTAND YOUR IDENTITY

And the Lord said unto Moses, See, I have made thee a god to Pharaoh: and Aaron thy brother shall be thy prophet. Thou shalt speak all that I command thee: and Aaron thy brother shall speak unto Pharaoh, that he send the children of Israel out of his land. And I will harden Pharaoh's heart, and multiply my signs and my wonders in the land of Egypt. But Pharaoh shall not hearken unto you, that I may lay my hand upon Egypt, and bring forth mine armies, and my people the children of Israel, out of the land of Egypt by great judgments. And the Egyptians shall know that I am the Lord, when I stretch forth mine hand upon Egypt, and bring out the children of Israel from among them. And Moses and Aaron did as the Lord commanded them, so did they. And Moses was fourscore years old, and Aaron fourscore and three years old, when they spake unto Pharaoh. And the Lord spake unto Moses and unto Aaron, saying, When Pharaoh shall speak unto you, saying, Shew a miracle for you: then thou shalt say unto Aaron, Take thy rod, and cast it before Pharaoh, and it shall become a serpent. And Moses and Aaron went in unto Pharaoh, and they did so as the Lord had commanded: and Aaron cast down his rod before

Pharaoh, and before his servants, and it became a serpent. Then Pharaoh also called the wise men and the sorcerers: now the magicians of Egypt, they also did in like manner with their enchantments. For they cast down every man his rod, and they became serpents: but Aaron's rod swallowed up their rods. And he hardened Pharaoh's heart, that he hearkened not unto them; as the Lord had said.

— EXODUS 7:1-13 (KJV)

I want to highlight what you need to know to prevail in every battle of life. In the original language, God said to Moses, *"I will make you Elohim."* It was Elohim saying, *"I will make you Elohim."*

> God presides over heaven's court; he pronounces judgment on the heavenly beings: "How long will you hand down unjust decisions by favoring the wicked? Give justice to the poor and the orphan; uphold the rights of the oppressed and the destitute. Rescue the poor and helpless; deliver them from the grasp of evil people. But these oppressors know nothing; they are so ignorant! They wander about in darkness, while the whole world is shaken to the core. I say, 'You are gods; you are all children of the Most High. But you will die like mere mortals and fall like every other ruler.'"
>
> — PSALM 82:1-7

God said the children of the Most High would die like mere mortals because they didn't know who they were. They didn't know who God had made them.

> The Lord said to my Lord, "Sit in the place of honor at my right hand until I humble your enemies, making them a footstool under your feet." The Lord will extend your powerful kingdom from Jerusalem; you will rule over your enemies.

> When you go to war, your people will serve you willingly. You are arrayed in holy garments, and your strength will be renewed each day like the morning dew. The Lord has taken an oath and will not break his vow: "You are a priest forever in the order of Melchizedek." The Lord stands at your right hand to protect you. He will strike down many kings when his anger erupts. He will punish the nations and fill their lands with corpses; he will shatter heads over the whole earth. But he himself will be refreshed from brooks along the way. He will be victorious.
>
> — PSALM 110:1-7

First, God said to Moses, *"I will make you Elohim."* Then He said to us, His children, *"I say, ye are gods and children of the Most High."* Then, in Psalm 110:1, *"The Lord said to my Lord."* In the original language, it means, *"Jehovah said my Jehovah."* He called Moses *"Elohim."* He said to His children, *"You are gods."* And then He called David *"Jehovah."*

You must understand who God says you are if you want to walk in victory. God conferred his own title three different times, once to Moses, once to David, and once to all His children:

> "The Father and I are one." Once again the people picked up stones to kill him. Jesus said, "At my Father's direction I have done many good works. For which one are you going to stone me?" They replied, "We're stoning you not for any good work, but for blasphemy! You, a mere man, claim to be God."
>
> — JOHN 10:30-33

In this scripture, Jesus claims that He's a God, and the people wanted to kill Him for claiming oneness with God. But Jesus didn't reply by telling them about His virgin birth in a manger. Jesus responded by quoting the same scripture you read above:

> Jesus replied, "It is written in your own Scriptures that God said to certain leaders of the people, 'I say, you are gods!' And you know that the Scriptures cannot be altered. So if those people who received God's message were called 'gods,' why do you call it blasphemy when I say, 'I am the Son of God'? After all, the Father set me apart and sent me into the world. Don't believe me unless I carry out my Father's work. But if I do his work, believe in the evidence of the miraculous works I have done, even if you don't believe me. Then you will know and understand that the Father is in me, and I am in the Father." Once again they tried to arrest him, but he got away and left them. He went beyond the Jordan River near the place where John was first baptizing and stayed there awhile. And many followed him. "John didn't perform miraculous signs," they remarked to one another, "but everything he said about this man has come true." And many who were there believed in Jesus.
>
> — JOHN 10:34-42

When they said it was blasphemy for Jesus to claim equality with God, He referred to their own law in Psalm 82. God said to certain leaders who had received His Word, *"Behold, I say ye are gods."*

If you're a minister, don't avoid preaching this. Neglecting this truth that *"ye are gods,"* has created a generation of worship songs sung from an unsaved perspective. Many don't believe Christ can live in them. Just read some of the bios and posts of Christians on social media. "I'm just a nobody trying to tell everybody about somebody," that's not in the Bible. "I'm just a beggar who found some bread, telling the other beggars where the bread is." This is not who the Bible says you are.

They call Him King of kings and Lord of lords because He's the Most High King of kings, and the Most High Lord, Elohim of elohims, Adonai of adonais, and Jehovah of jehovahs, according to the Bible. I didn't find one obscure scripture to present to you. I didn't just read it three times in the Old Testament; Jesus used the exact interpretation to claim equality with God. As He said, *"The Scriptures can't be broken."*

> My old self has been crucified with Christ. It is no longer I who live, but Christ lives in me. So I live in this earthly body by trusting in the Son of God, who loved me and gave himself for me.
>
> — GALATIANS 2:20

The Bible teaches that the love of God is shed abroad in your heart, not on the outside trailing behind you. He lives in you. You either understand that Christ lives in you, or you end up a washed-up, defeated American believer. You'll find out that some people enjoy being defeated. They enjoy being on the prayer requests list. They enjoy writing despondent Facebook posts. Some people are not interested in entering into victory, but if you're reading this, you are interested.

> Herein is our love made perfect, that we may have boldness in the day of judgment: because as he is, so are we in this world.
>
> — 1 JOHN 4:17 (KJV)

As Christ is now, so are we in this world. According to Finis Dake's reference Bible, the Christian must:

- Be free from the cares of this world.
- Not gain the world at the expense of his soul.
- Not offend others as the world does.
- Not be of the world.
- Not love his life in the world.
- Be delivered from the world.
- Be crucified to the world.
- Shine his light as a light in the world.
- Deny its lusts, and live godly in the world.

- Be unspotted from the world.
- Not be friends with the world.
- Escape the pollution and corruption of the world.
- Not love the world, or the things that are in the world.
- Be like Christ in the world.
- Overcome the world.
- Be chosen out of the world.
- Be not conformed to the world.
- Be dead to its ways.[i]

You may think what I'm teaching is too strong, but when people don't speak the unadulterated Word, they gravitate in the opposite direction toward sin and defeat. You must pick one or the other: either believe what the Bible says or go with that new American gospel that teaches we all sin daily. That's not what the Bible teaches.

When you reject what the Bible says, you gravitate toward the acceptance of defeat, sin, and failure. Understand that God has made you of Him, it's no longer you who's alive, it's Christ who lives in you, and Christ is God. Your life is now God's life on the inside of you. The mind of Christ is in you. God's Spirit is inside of you: God's tongue, God's hand, and God's feet. Where you go, God goes. What you speak, God says.

20 REASONS TO REFUSE TO LIVE IN SIN

1. You've died to sin, so it's nullified.
2. You've been resurrected from spiritual death.
3. You walk in the newness of life.
4. Death to sin and resurrection from sin means walking like Christ.
5. The old man is crucified and dead.
6. The body of sin is destroyed, henceforth, you should not sin.
7. You are freed from sin.
8. Faith counts sin as paid debt.

9. Sin has no dominion over you.
10. Sin should not reign in the body.
11. The body must not yield to sin.
12. You are married to Christ, not to sin.
13. You walk in the Spirit.
14. You are made free from the law of sin.
15. You are spiritually minded.
16. Christ is in you, not sin.
17. You are not debtors to sin.
18. The Spirit mortifies the sin in you or puts the sin to death.
19. You have the spirit of freedom.
20. The intercession of Christ and the Holy Spirit keeps you pure.[ii]

As He is, so are we in this world. As Jesus is right now, so am I in this world. When you speak, Jesus is speaking. When you lay your hands on people, Jesus is laying His hands on them. Where you go, Jesus goes. That's the message of the Bible. You and Christ are now one.

You have become one with God by birth. John 3:6 says, *"Whatever is born of the flesh is flesh, but whatever is born of the spirit is spirit."* You are not a human being trying to live a spiritual life. You are a spirit being, trying to relate to people who are below. Jesus said, *"You are from below, I'm from above"* (John 8:23). Therefore, *"As He is, so are we in this world"* (1 John 4:17). We've passed from death into life. We've been transferred out of this carnal realm into the spirit realm. We don't go from mountains to valleys; we are seated with Christ in heavenly places, far above. By birth, we have been born of God. The Bible says in 1 John 5:4, *"Whatsoever is born of God overcomes the world. This is the victory that overcomes the world, even our faith."*

I'm born of God. I'm God's son. The Bible refers to Jesus as our Elder Brother. Think of that. You're not different from your brother. My sister, Jessica, is not a goldfish. We're of the same species and likeness. You don't have children born into a family where one is a human being, one is a dog, and one is a cat. No, they're born of their father. If a cat has a son, it's a cat. If a dog has a son, it's a dog. If an elephant has a son, it's an elephant. If I have a son, he's a man. When God produces a son, His son is also a god. Those are the laws of reproduction, the laws of nature, and the laws of the Bible. Everything produces after its kind. That's why God called Moses "Elohim," called David "Jehovah," and said to those who received the word, *"I say ye are gods,"* and Jesus said, *"I and the Father are one."* Now declare this:

 I'm of God by birth and I'm of God by marriage.

My wife's name used to be Adalis Ortiz. When she married me, she became Adalis Shuttlesworth. She took my name because when a bride marries a husband—unless they're an ultra-feminist—they take their husband's last name. The Bible calls us the bride of Christ. We took His name, His nature, and His likeness. We've been married into His family. The Bible says in marriage two become one flesh. That's not a stretch either because the Bible says, *"And don't you realize that if a man joins himself to a prostitute, he becomes one body with her? For the Scriptures say, 'The two are united into one. But the person who is joined to the Lord is one spirit with him"* (1 Corinthians 6:16-17). As the bride of Christ, we have taken His name, and by birth, we've taken His nature.

Now that we're born of God and have His nature and likeness, what does it mean?

> Well then, should we keep on sinning so that God can show us more and more of his wonderful grace? Of course not! Since we have died to sin, how can we continue to live in it? Or have you forgotten that when we were joined with Christ Jesus in baptism, we joined him in his death? For we died and were buried with Christ by baptism. And just as Christ was raised from the dead by the glorious power of the Father, now we also may live new lives. Since we have been united with him in his death, we will also be raised to life as he was. We know that our old sinful selves were crucified with Christ so that sin might lose its power in our lives. We are no longer slaves to sin. For when we died with Christ we were set free

> from the power of sin. And since we died with Christ, we know we will also live with him. We are sure of this because Christ was raised from the dead, and he will never die again. Death no longer has any power over him. When he died, he died once to break the power of sin. But now that he lives, he lives for the glory of God.
>
> — ROMANS 6:1-10

Consider yourself dead to the power of sin and alive under God through Christ Jesus. What you think of yourself matters. Imagine the power in saying: "I am dead to sin and alive under God through Christ Jesus."

> Do not let sin control the way you live; do not give in to sinful desires. Do not let any part of your body become an instrument of evil to serve sin. Instead, give yourselves completely to God, for you were dead, but now you have new life. So use your whole body as an instrument to do what is right for the glory of God.
>
> — ROMANS 6:12-13

The Revised Geneva Translation of Romans 6 says, *"And give the parts of your body to God, as weapons of righteousness. For sin shall not have dominion over you."* According to the Bible, you never have to sin one time. You can choose to, but you don't have to.

> Whosoever is born of God doth not commit sin; for his seed remaineth in him: and he cannot sin, because he is born of God.
>
> — 1 JOHN 3:9 (KJV)

JONATHAN SHUTTLESWORTH

WHAT DOES IT MEAN TO BE ONE WITH GOD?

1. You're righteous as Christ is righteous.

God's seed is in us. He put His righteousness in us. Many of us grew up in a church where we were always taught to be conscious of sin, and it resulted in many people feeling stuck in sin. Those born of God do not sin because His seed remains in them. They cannot make a practice of sinning. The Bible says you are the righteousness of God in Christ. You are righteous just as Christ is righteous. You're not a dirty sinner trying to gain God's approval. God's seed and His righteousness are in you if you've surrendered your life to Jesus.

2. You have His Spirit.

> All praise to God, the Father of our Lord Jesus Christ, who has blessed us with every spiritual blessing in the heavenly realms because we are united with Christ.
>
> — EPHESIANS 1:3

> And now you Gentiles have also heard the truth, the Good News that God saves you. And when you believed in Christ, he identified you as his own by giving you the Holy Spirit, whom he promised long ago. The Spirit is God's guarantee that he will give us the inheritance he promised and that he has purchased us to be his own people. He did this so we would praise and glorify him. Ever since I first heard of your strong faith in the Lord Jesus and your love for God's people everywhere, I have not stopped thanking God for you. I pray for you constantly, asking God, the glorious Father of our Lord Jesus Christ, to give you spiritual wisdom and insight so that you might grow in your knowledge of God. I pray that your hearts will be flooded with light so that you can understand the confident hope he has given to those he called—his holy people who are his rich and glorious inheritance. I also

> pray that you will understand the incredible greatness of God's power for us who believe him. This is the same mighty power that raised Christ from the dead and seated him in the place of honor at God's right hand in the heavenly realms. Now he is far above any ruler or authority or power or leader or anything else—not only in this world but also in the world to come. God has put all things under the authority of Christ and has made him head over all things for the benefit of the church. And the church is his body; it is made full and complete by Christ, who fills all things everywhere with himself.
>
> — EPHESIANS 1:13-23

God's powerful Spirit is in you. You don't have a weak spirit. You're not operating with a human spirit. God has given you His Holy Spirit as a foretaste of what you'll receive through inheritance. You can operate as Christ operates. You have His righteousness. You're not a sinner. You don't have to sin. You're righteous, and you can choose to use your body as a weapon of righteousness. Your spirit is the Lord's Spirit. *"He who's joined to the Lord has become one spirit with Him"* (1 Corinthians 6:17). None of these Scriptures are taken out of context. They can be found in both the Old and New Testaments. The whole teaching of the New Testament is rooted in the understanding that you operate as He is on this Earth.

Philip was caught up and disappeared after baptizing the Ethiopian eunuch, but he wasn't operating in human power. He had become as God on the Earth, and that power is available to everyone, including you.

Religion wants you to believe Jesus is chasing after you. "How many know, no matter how much we sin, He still loves us." I'm not sinning. I'm not an unbeliever. I'm not telling you what religion expects you to do. My life is wrapped up in doing God's will. I want no part of lukewarm American Christianity. I'm not in that club. I'm not at the bar. No one is in my bed other than my wife. *"He who sins is of the devil, for the devil has sinned from the beginning"* (1 John 3:8), but our righteousness has a visible expression. Ephesians 1 says we have His Spirit and power on the inside of us.

3. You have His mind.

> For who hath known the mind of the Lord, that he may instruct Him? But we have the mind of Christ.
>
> — 1 CORINTHIANS 2:16 (KJV)

When Paul asked who can know what the Lord is thinking, and who can instruct Him, he was asking, "What unspiritual man can instruct the spiritual man?" We don't have to run what we believe by CNN or the New York Times. They operate on a lower mental plane. The Christian operates by a supernatural mind.

Christ wasn't an idiot. In John 6, when the disciples said: *"These people need food, what are we supposed to do?"* Jesus always knew what to do. Every time they sent lawyers or teachers of the religious law to trick Jesus, His answers would baffle them and shame His enemies.

If you've been told that you have a learning problem, that might've been true before you were saved, but now you have a new mind. The Bible says you must consider yourself that way for it to manifest. If you call yourself stupid, you'll be stupid. If you say you have trouble remembering things, you'll have trouble remembering things. But if you start saying, "Thank You, Lord, that I have the mind of Christ, that Your supernatural mind operates in me. I can out-think my opponents, in Jesus' name," it'll manifest.

4. Your body carries God's glory.

"Know ye not you're the temple of the Holy Ghost?" (1 Corinthians 6:19). Paul's clothes were taken to those who were sick, and any sickness or disease was healed, and evil spirits left. That's not a man operating; that's God operating in a man. This dominion is not only recognized in the Bible and in Heaven, this dominion is also recognized by the Devil. He knows

those who operate in this dominion. When you know who you are and live holy instead of worldly, it's known in Hell. The demon in Acts 19:15 essentially told those rogue, un-Spirit-filled guys, "If you were Jesus or Paul, we would have left, but we know you don't have what they carry." Whatever is born of God overcomes the world. Now that we are born of God, we have dominion.

PART III
YOUR OFFENSIVE WEAPONS

CHAPTER 10

JESUS THE ROD: YOUR SOURCE OF POWER

And the Lord said unto Moses, See, I have made thee a god to Pharaoh: and Aaron thy brother shall be thy prophet. Thou shalt speak all that I command thee: and Aaron thy brother shall speak unto Pharaoh, that he send the children of Israel out of his land. And I will harden Pharaoh's heart, and multiply my signs and my wonders in the land of Egypt. But Pharaoh shall not hearken unto you, that I may lay my hand upon Egypt, and bring forth mine armies, and my people the children of Israel, out of the land of Egypt by great judgments. And the Egyptians shall know that I am the Lord, when I stretch forth mine hand upon Egypt, and bring out the children of Israel from among them.

— EXODUS 7:1-5 (KJV)

It's important to note the original text. *"I have made you a god in God's stead."* The Hebrew word used for *God* in Exodus 7:1 is *Elohim*. Elohim refers to men who were to act in God's place before men. It is a word that denotes Divine authority—the power to rule.

> But Pharaoh shall not hearken unto you, that I may lay my hand upon Egypt, and bring forth mine armies, and my people the children of Israel, out of the land of Egypt by great judgments. And the Egyptians shall know that I am the Lord, when I stretch forth mine hand upon Egypt, and bring out the children of Israel from among them. And Moses and Aaron did as the Lord commanded them, so did they. And Moses was fourscore years old, and Aaron fourscore and three years old, when they spake unto Pharaoh. And the Lord spake unto Moses and unto Aaron, saying, When Pharaoh shall speak unto you, saying, Shew a miracle for you: then thou shalt say unto Aaron, Take thy rod, and cast it before Pharaoh, and it shall become a serpent. And Moses and Aaron went in unto Pharaoh, and they did so as the Lord had commanded: and Aaron cast down his rod before Pharaoh, and before his servants, and it became a serpent. Then Pharaoh also called the wise men and the sorcerers: now the magicians of Egypt, they also did in like manner with their enchantments. For they cast down every man his rod, and they became serpents: but Aaron's rod swallowed up their rods.
>
> — EXODUS 7:4-12 (KJV)

Finis Dake noted that the rods of the magicians became serpents, but Aaron's swallowed up the others, proving that God's power is greater than Satan's.[i]

> And there shall come forth a rod out of the stem of Jesse, and a Branch shall grow out of his roots: And the spirit of the Lord shall rest upon, the spirit of wisdom and understanding, the spirit of counsel and might, the spirit of knowledge and of the fear of the Lord; And shall make him of quick understanding in the fear of the Lord.
>
> — ISAIAH 11:1-3 (KJV)

Again, according to Dake's reference Bible, this refers to a full-grown and strong rod cut from a tree and capable of being used to beat out grain, correct children, shepherd flocks, rule over a kingdom as a king's scepter, and a strong club for war and protection.[ii]

This is a messianic prophecy referring to Jesus. They were given a literal rod. When they threw it down, it became a serpent and swallowed up the rods of the magicians—it ate the Devil's power. They didn't even have any rods left. The Bible says Jesus is that Rod for us. What occurred with Moses and Aaron in the Old Covenant is a type of what we have now. Christ is our Rod. When we invoke His power, it swallows up the Devil's power and every tactic of the Devil sent against your life. God didn't just make us His children. He gave us a Rod. It's not just for correction, it's also for protection, and to rule now in the midst of your enemies.

> The Lord said unto my Lord, Sit thou at My right hand, until I make thine enemies thy footstool. The Lord shall send the rod of thy strength out of Zion: rule Thou in the midst of Thine enemies.
>
> — PSALM 110:1-2 (KJV)

There it is again—in the original Hebrew text, God refers to His servant with His name: "Elohim," the same name God used when He addressed Moses. Psalm 110:1 says, *"The Lord said unto my Lord,"* God called David *"my Jehovah."* God used that terminology. This is where you cross the bridge from religion into Bible Christianity—or not. We are as God. If you disconnect from Him, you can do nothing, but when you connect with God, He calls you by His name.

When a bride is married, she takes her husband's name. When you are born of God, you are married to Christ and you take His name. Imagine the power in calling yourself the names God has called you.

God called Moses Elohim under an old covenant. In the new covenant, we have Jesus, who shed His blood and tore the veil in two. We have a better covenant based on better promises. When the Bible says, *"The*

Lord shall send the rod of Thy strength out of Zion. Rule now in the midst of Thine enemies," God gave Moses the rod. Christ is the rod that came out of the stem of Jesse and was given to us. That's why Exodus refers to multiple serpents, and the rod of Aaron swallowed up all the other serpents. Now declare this:

 I rule now in the midst of my enemies.

You will face enemies, but the rod God gave us doesn't allow them to rule over us. When you use it, it gives you the power to rule over the surrounding enemies.

If you're wondering how Jesus could be a rod that turned into a serpent or why God would tell Moses to throw down the rod for it to become a snake, allow me to explain. Snakes always typify the demonic. The Bible says, *"You'll trample on snakes and scorpions"* (Luke 10:19). Christ became sin, swallowed up the curse around us, and then became our rod again. The rod that Aaron held typifies Christ in us, allowing us to rule in the midst of our enemies. Your enemies cannot rule over you unless you let them. God gave you dominion and power to rule amid your enemies.

So how do you rule over your enemies practically? You study the Bible and identify everything it refers to as an enemy. Sickness is an enemy. The Bible says death is the last enemy to be destroyed (1 Corinthians 15:26). You have dominion over sickness and death.

Poverty is an enemy. Poverty is an instrument of death. If you become poor enough, you die. People don't understand this in America because the poor receive help from the government or a soup kitchen. But when you run out of money in other countries, you can't afford to eat and then you die. There's no aid to help you. Poverty is an enemy.

Depression is another enemy. Everything that comes against your joy is an enemy. Everything that comes against your success is an enemy.

You don't have to call someone who knows Christ to pray for you—you know Christ. Carry the rod. Invoke the power to rule in the midst of your enemies.

Your mouth is the primary channel to release the power of God and rule amid your enemies. Open your mouth and speak. If you sit still when your enemy attacks, you'll lose or die. Aaron had to throw down the rod. There's an action you must take to throw down the power and have it swallow up your opposition.

> Is not this the fast that I have chosen? To loose the bands of wickedness, to undo the heavy burdens, and to let the oppressed go free, and that ye break every yoke? Is it not to deal thy bread to the hungry, and that thou bring the poor that are cast out to thy house? When thou seest the naked, that thou cover him; and that thou hide not thyself from thine own flesh? Then shall thy light break forth as the morning, and thine health shall spring forth speedily: and thy righteousness shall go before thee; the glory of the Lord shall be thy reward. Then shalt thou call, and the Lord shall answer; thou shalt cry, and he shall say, Here I am. If thou take away from the midst of thee the yoke, the putting forth of the finger, and speaking vanity.
>
> — ISAIAH 58:6-9 (KJV)

Most people don't have a problem believing God. The common issue in the lives of Christians is that they don't know how to release God's power in their lives.

In Exodus 14, God freed the Israelites from Egyptian captivity, but the Egyptian army pursued them to pull them back into slavery. Many people are confused by the attempts of the Devil to pull them back into captivity. The Devil was forced to turn you loose, but if you allow him to, he'll take you back. You must take action to secure your victory.

> But Moses told the people, "Don't be afraid. Just stand still and watch the Lord rescue you today. The Egyptians you see today will never be seen again. The Lord himself will fight for you. Just stay calm."
>
> — EXODUS 14:13-14

This sounds great, but the story doesn't end here. God rebuked Moses in the next verse.

> Then the Lord said to Moses, "Why are you crying out to me?"
>
> — EXODUS 14:15

That's what God says every time you drag Him into a situation. "I gave *you* My power. I gave *you* My authority. It's up to you to use it." When you ask God to do something He already gave you the power and authority to accomplish, it's like a policeman who sees someone robbing a 7-Eleven and says boldly, "Wait until the mayor hears about this! You're going to be in a lot of trouble, mister." Actually, when the mayor and the chief of police find out, that policeman will be the one in trouble. He'll end up reprimanded or fired because it's his job to enforce the laws the mayor has passed.

God has passed the laws. It's our responsibility to enforce them. We have a badge—the authority of God's Word—and we have a weapon for whatever and whoever doesn't respect the badge. In these next few chapters, I will show you how to use your weapon.

Satan is a thief. Thieves take what is not theirs. Thieves go where they're not allowed to go. That's easy to understand. Why do people get confused and surprised when the Devil attacks? If you don't know how to attack back, you're going to be in a world of hurt your entire life.

Renowned Pentecostal preacher John G. Lake preached a message entitled *Moses' Rebuke*. He preached how Moses was given a rod by God and said, "Whatever you do and say, I will make you as God to the Egyptians. I will make you as God to the Israelites." Moses tried to back out of that arrangement and pawn it back on God, and in response, God asked Moses, *"Why are you crying out to Me? Stretch forth your hand and divide the water."*

People struggle for long periods of time because they do what Moses did in Exodus. God didn't give us a wooden rod, but the Bible says that Jesus is the rod that proceeds out of the stem of Jesse, and He lives in us. He gave us that rod, and there are specific ways He expects us to use it.

Any thief trespassing or attempting to steal from you, who does not respect your badge, will respect your weapon: the power of the Holy Ghost. Claiming to believe in God and trust in Him is not a weapon. When you trust God, you act in faith and it releases the power. It will change your life. When you put these Bible truths into practice, you will prevail in every battle of life. You won't need people to pray for you. You won't be perpetually on your church's prayer request list. God didn't create you to be a community prayer project. God created you to bring solutions to the world, not for people to bring solutions to you.

If your mouth works and there's faith in your heart, you will have victory over the enemy. If your heart isn't filled with faith, fill it up with the Word, then open your mouth and pray. We don't need Christians who continually feed at the breast of religious leaders. We need a new generation of Christians who know how to go boldly before God's throne and provoke God's power to bring change. I see you taking that place, in Jesus' name!

> Then the Lord said to Moses, "Why are you crying out to me? Tell the people to get moving! Pick up your staff and raise your hand over the sea. Divide the water so the Israelites can walk through the middle of the sea on dry ground. And I will harden the hearts of the Egyptians, and they will charge in after the Israelites. My great glory will be displayed through Pharaoh and his troops, his chariots, and his charioteers. When my glory is displayed through them, all Egypt will see my glory and know that I am the Lord!"
>
> — EXODUS 14:15-18

Everything God does involves equal parts the hand of God and the hand of man. When Moses told the Israelites God would fight for them, God reminded them it was their responsibility to use the rod He gave them to wield His power and perform signs.

> And there shall come forth a Rod out of the stem of Jesse, and a Branch shall grow out of his roots: And the spirit of the Lord shall rest upon him, the spirit of wisdom and understanding, the spirit of counsel and might, the spirit of knowledge and of the fear of the Lord; And shall make him of quick understanding in the fear of the Lord: and he shall not judge after the sight of his eyes, neither reprove after the hearing of his ears.
>
> — ISAIAH 11:1-3 (KJV)

The Bible says Jesus is the Rod that comes out of the stem of Jesse. It's a messianic prophecy. Isaiah chapter 11 refers to power when it says, *"And the spirit of the Lord shall rest upon him."* Christ in us, the hope of glory, is our Rod.

In the Old Testament, everything was physical—they killed actual people. In the New Testament, it's spiritual. Christ gave us His Spirit to live within us. He is the Rod given to Moses, the Rod we are to use to do signs. Grasp that. When Moses tried to back out of his deal with God, he was told: *"Moses, I will make you like God to Pharaoh. Now take this rod and with it do signs."* Authority has been granted to us the same way it was given to Moses, only better. We've been given a rod; Christ is the Rod that proceeds out of the stem of Jesse.

We're to take what He's given us and provoke the signs, not wait for God to do them. God is waiting for you to do it, and there are four primary channels to release God's power. We have a badge—the authority of God's Word—and we have a weapon for whatever doesn't respect the badge. In the next few chapters, we'll examine four primary ways to use the weapon God gave you to enforce the badge you have on your chest.

CHAPTER 11

YOUR MOUTH

I hear two different views preached in Christianity. In America, they preach: "We might be driving home from church tonight, a car could cross the double yellow lines, and our life would be required of us. We would die and stand before the Lord. Would you be ready to meet Him?" They always spin it in such a way that life is left to chance, and we could die at any time.

But there's another view I developed as a child. I read the parts of the Bible that said, *"With long life will I satisfy you and show you my salvation"* (Psalm 91:16). *"Children, honor your mother and father (for this is the first commandment with a promise) that your days will be long on the earth"* (Ephesians 6:1-3). I learned from reading the Bible that there are things I can do to shorten my life, and there are things I can do to lengthen it.

A DOCTRINE THAT OVERTHROWS THE OPPOSITION

I've met ministers from Nigeria who overthrew Islamic Jihadists and today pastor booming churches. I noticed they didn't have a doctrine that accepted defeat. They had solid Biblical doctrine that refused to put up with the Devil's harassment. A doctrine that produced men and women who viewed themselves as a force aligned against the Devil and refused to allow him to trample over them. I began to listen and study that viewpoint. It's clearly found in the scriptures we've reviewed so far. Which line of thinking makes more sense to you?

Jana Pauls—the missionary who travels worldwide—comes to my mind when I explain this first weapon. I first encountered her in one of my meetings in East London, South Africa. I called her out in the meeting and told her, "God didn't call you to die. God called you to preach. You'll do more for God alive than dead." She broke down and started crying. She had been telling everybody, "I feel called to go preach in the Middle East, and I'm ready to die. I know I'm going to go there and die."

God didn't call you to die, and He didn't call me to die. An angel didn't visit me in my room when I was eight years old to say, "Jonathan, you're to die a premature death." No, he said, "I want you to preach." You can't preach when you're dead. You have all of eternity to be in Heaven. You have a limited amount of time to impact your generation with the Gospel of Jesus Christ while you're alive on the Earth.

What I saw in the Bible made me believe differently. The Bible instructs us to *"Imitate those who through faith and patience inherit the promises"* (Hebrews 6:12). *"You will know them by their fruits"* (Matthew 7:16). Believing and declaring "I'm ready to die at any time," will produce premature death. People who talk that way don't travel to preach and drive Islam out of a nation; Islam drives them out of their nation—the two can't coexist. One looks to drive the other out: Islam by violence, Christianity by love and salvation. That's how it works. When I watched that preaching in action overseas, I saw the fruit produced by resisting the Devil—it captures nations for Christ.

Whether you've been saved for six months or sixty years, you've probably heard people say, "We're really going through a hard time, but I'm trusting Jesus." People preach about the storms of life that rage and instruct their congregants to just sit back and trust Jesus. That's not how the Bible teaches us to deal with storms. This is how Jesus dealt with storms:

> As evening came, Jesus said to his disciples, "Let's cross to the other side of the lake." So they took Jesus in the boat and started out, leaving the crowds behind (although other boats followed). But soon a fierce storm came up. High waves were breaking into the boat, and it began to fill with water. Jesus was sleeping at the back of the boat with his head on a cushion. The disciples woke him up, shouting, "Teacher, don't you care that we're going to drown?" When Jesus woke up, he rebuked the wind.
>
> — MARK 4:35-39

Rebuking is no longer a common practice in North America. People don't rebuke their children or anyone else, but it's an instruction you must follow to resist the Devil. *"Every tongue which rises against you in judgment you shall condemn. This is the heritage of the servants of the Lord"* (Isaiah 54:17). If you don't speak to the storm, it'll sink your ship. Open your mouth and use your tongue like the weapon it is. It's not a weapon meant to destroy you or your family—it's a weapon that destroys whatever the enemy has sent to destroy you.

> When Jesus woke up, he rebuked the wind and said to the waves, "Silence! Be still!" Suddenly the wind stopped, and there was a great calm. Then he asked them, "Why are you afraid? Do you still have no faith?" The disciples were absolutely terrified. "Who is this man?" they asked each other. "Even the wind and waves obey him!"
>
> — MARK 4:39-41

God rebuked Moses, and Jesus rebuked His disciples for coming to Him when He had already told them what to do. There was an action that man had to take. Christ acted and Moses had to act. If you don't act, there's no way for God to get involved in your outcome.

The tongue is a weapon. Your words have creative and destructive power. Instead of just randomly saying things and haphazardly creating a destructive reality, why not use your mouth the way God intended it, as a weapon of righteousness?

The Bible instructs in Romans 6 to use your whole body as a weapon of righteousness.

> The Lord took hold of me, and I was carried away by the Spirit of the Lord to a valley filled with bones. He led me all around among the bones that covered the valley floor. They were scattered everywhere across the ground and were completely dried out. Then he asked me, "Son of man, can these bones become living people again?" "O Sovereign Lord," I replied, "you alone know the answer to that." Then he said to me, "Speak a prophetic message to these bones and say, 'Dry bones, listen to the word of the Lord! This is what the Sovereign Lord says: Look! I am going to put breath into you and make you live again! I will put flesh and muscles on you and cover you with skin. I will put breath into you, and you will come to life. Then you will know that I am the Lord.'" So I spoke this message, just as he told me. Suddenly as I spoke, there was a rattling noise all across the valley. The bones of each body came together and attached themselves as complete skeletons. Then as I watched, muscles and flesh formed over the bones. Then skin formed to cover their bodies, but they still had no breath in them. Then he said to me, "Speak a prophetic message to the winds, son of man. Speak a prophetic message and say, 'This is what the Sovereign Lord says: Come, O breath, from the four winds! Breathe into these dead bodies so they may live again.'" So I spoke the message as he commanded me, and breath came into their bodies. They all came to life and stood up on their feet—a great army.
>
> — EZEKIEL 37:1-10

God didn't instruct Ezekiel to sit back and watch Him bring the dry bones to life. He gave Ezekiel the words to speak, and then God acted to carry out the spoken words. Everything with God operates by believing it in your heart and confessing with your mouth. Ezekiel had to believe what God told him. Then, he had to believe it enough to speak to the bones and command them to live again. If Ezekiel didn't believe it, he wouldn't have been used by God. He could have chosen to say, "C'mon God, let's be realistic," but he took God at His word. When he acted on what God said, it caused that valley of dry bones to rattle together. Flesh, muscle, and sinew were produced, and then he spoke again for breath to come into the bodies.

God instructed people to speak all throughout the Bible. Joshua commanded the sun to stand still. He spoke it first, then there was rattling, and it began to manifest. God needs you to speak what He said. You must speak to dry bones and speak to the storm.

A while ago, after I'd finished preaching at a youth camp, I went to sit down. Having ministered for two and a half hours while on a 21-day fast, I was finished for the night. A guy came over to me and asked, "Can you pray for this girl over here? She's one of my youth leaders, and she's having a panic attack."

She was shaking and saying, "I'm so afraid,"—it was a full-out demonic attack.

"She's one of your youth leaders?" I asked.

"Yes," he replied.

"You're a youth pastor?"

"Yes."

"You went to Bible school for four years?" I asked.

"Yes."

"Then you do it," I said.

He looked annoyed.

"Why are you in the ministry? She's your leader, you can't take authority over that?"

He walked over to the girl, visibly upset that I had told him to address the issue himself. He put one hand on her back and his other arm in the air and said, "Peace, peace, peace," while she continued to shake. That's not how you get rid of a demon. So, after the youth leader made it clear he had no idea what he was doing, I stood in front of her, put my hands on her head, and said, "You foul spirit of fear, turn loose this woman now!" and it stopped. She hugged me as I commanded it to never come back.

I had a few words for that youth pastor after I finished. I told him that if he's going to be in the ministry, he should learn how to take authority over problems. A plumber doesn't need to consult another plumber to fix a sink. A roofer doesn't need to ask another roofer how to fix a roof. A pastor should not need another pastor to access the power of God to set people free. People suffer because leaders have a form of godliness but deny the power. They've traded the release of power that God gave us for a religious act and ritual that doesn't work. When someone needs prayer for a sickness or disease, the first word out of your mouth shouldn't be "Father." God isn't at the root of sickness. You speak to the foul spirit and command it to leave in the name of Jesus and destroy it.

People are rarely taught how to speak to the storm. Christians love to recite religious platitudes like, "Don't talk to God about how big your mountain is; talk to your mountain about how big your God is." That's not in the Bible. Stick to what the Bible says. Jesus never said, "You can speak to any mountain and tell it how great your God is, and then God will move the mountain." He said *you* must speak to the mountain and tell it to move, and *your* command will be obeyed. Open your mouth and speak. Jesus didn't say, "In My name, you'll talk to God about demons." He said, *"In My name*, you *will cast out devils"* (Mark 16:17). *You* speak to the demon.

There's a growing soft temperament in people these days, especially in church leadership. Pastors will stand up in front of their congregations, pray a weak, defeated prayer for a dozen names on a prayer list, and then do it all over again the following week for the same people because no one is ever healed. There's no violence in their spirit. You must attack with your words.

When Jesus spoke to the storm, He used strong words in the Aramaic language. He said, "Shut up!"—the harshest shut up in the original language. He did not softly utter, "Peace, be still."

Smith Wigglesworth said, "Satan's not a gentleman, so you don't treat him as one." He understands one language, and that's the language of boldness and power. Speak that way, it makes a difference.

> Death and life are in the power of the tongue. They that indulge therein shall enjoy the fruit thereof.
>
> — PROVERBS 18:21 (KJV)

You decide whether you'll have life or death. Ezekiel 37 proves that your words can be creative or destructive.

In Numbers 13, the twelve spies Moses sent to scout out the Promised Land returned, and after acknowledging how bountiful the land was, ten of the twelve spies immediately described the opposition. They were worried about the giants who lived there and even went so far as insisting that the giants looked at them as if they were grasshoppers. They spread what the Bible calls "an evil report of unbelief." But Joshua and Caleb tried to focus the people on the goodness of the land and the faith they had in God to deliver the land into their hands, and the people threatened to stone them.

> Then Moses and Aaron fell face down on the ground before the whole community of Israel. Two of the men who had explored the land, Joshua son of Nun and Caleb son of Jephunneh, tore their clothing. They said to all the people of Israel, "The land we traveled through and explored is a wonderful land! And if the Lord is pleased with us, he will bring us safely into that land and give it to us. It is a rich land flowing with milk and honey. Do not rebel against the Lord, and don't be afraid of the people of the land. They are only helpless prey to us! They have no protection, but the Lord is with us! Don't be afraid of them!" But the whole community

began to talk about stoning Joshua and Caleb. Then the glorious presence of the Lord appeared to all the Israelites at the Tabernacle.

— NUMBERS 14:5-10

People who live in unbelief get angry at people who have faith. Look how denominations treated Brother Kenneth Hagin. If they could have gotten away with it, they would've stoned him. Instead, they blasted him verbally every chance they had. Meanwhile, they died early of disease, and Brother Hagin preached the Gospel into his eighties.

I've made my choice. I'm not on the fence. I don't act denominational when I'm around denominational people, and faith and Holy Ghost when I'm around faith and Holy Ghost people. I'm a faith man, I'm a Holy Ghost man, and I believe in the Word of God. I speak the Word of God. If it ruffles religious people's feathers, they can kiss off. I'm not interested in pleasing them. I aim to please God. I will give an account for every idle or unproductive word that comes out of my mouth. I will speak words that make Jesus Christ stand up and clap in Heaven. I will speak words that prompt the likes of Smith Wigglesworth and those who went before me to say, "Keep saying that." God is not interested in wimpy language. We can declare a thing. He gave us the authority to decree a thing and see it be established (Job 22:28).

It was God's will that every Israelite enter the Promised Land, but only two families were permitted to enter. Two families out of an estimated 1.3 to 3.1 million people, depending on which Bible scholar you believe. If you don't line your mouth up with what God said, you will never taste your promised land.

> "...not one of these people will ever enter that land. They have all seen my glorious presence and the miraculous signs I performed both in Egypt and in the wilderness, but again and again they have tested me by refusing to listen to my voice. They will never even see the land I swore to give their ancestors. None of those who have treated me with contempt

will ever see it. But my servant Caleb has a different attitude than the others have. He has remained loyal to me, so I will bring him into the land he explored. His descendants will possess their full share of that land. Now turn around, and don't go on toward the land where the Amalekites and Canaanites live. Tomorrow you must set out for the wilderness in the direction of the Red Sea."

— NUMBERS 14:22-25

The only punishment for those who said, "We're not able to take the land," was they were granted exactly what they said. *"Now tell them this: 'As surely as I live, declares the Lord, I will do to you the very things I heard you say'"* (Numbers 14:28).

Some people believe their problem is the Devil, but their tongue does a better job of ruining their lives than the Devil ever could. As far as you're concerned, death and life are not in God's hands and they're not in the Devil's hands. Death and life are in the power of *your* tongue. The Devil wants to steal from, kill, and destroy every human on Earth, yet I'm not stolen from, killed, or destroyed. Whatever Satan wants for my life can't happen unless I line my mouth up with what the Devil says. When God likes what you say, your life will bear proof of it. Your words have the power to destroy or bring life. Don't walk around telling everyone it's flu season, and then act shocked when you come down with the flu. You get what you speak.

Caleb didn't speak like everyone else; He spoke like God and God liked it. Look at what happened to Joshua and Caleb forty-five years later.

> A delegation from the tribe of Judah, led by Caleb son of Jephunneh the Kenizzite, came to Joshua at Gilgal. Caleb said to Joshua, "Remember what the Lord said to Moses, the man of God, about you and me when we were at Kadesh-barnea. I was forty years old when Moses, the servant of the Lord, sent me from Kadesh-barnea to explore the land of Canaan. I returned and gave an honest

> report, but my brothers who went with me frightened the people from entering the Promised Land. For my part, I wholeheartedly followed the Lord my God. So that day Moses solemnly promised me, 'The land of Canaan on which you were just walking will be your grant of land and that of your descendants forever, because you wholeheartedly followed the Lord my God.' "Now, as you can see, the Lord has kept me alive and well as he promised for all these forty-five years since Moses made this promise—even while Israel wandered in the wilderness. Today I am eighty-five years old. I am as strong now as I was when Moses sent me on that journey, and I can still travel and fight as well as I could then. So give me the hill country that the Lord promised me. You will remember that as scouts we found the descendants of Anak living there in great, walled towns. But if the Lord is with me, I will drive them out of the land, just as the Lord said."
>
> — JOSHUA 14:6-12

Caleb spoke words of faith at forty years old and he continued to speak faith at eighty-five years old, as he took his most significant act of faith. You don't see too many people climbing mountains at eighty-five years old. Your words will determine your life. *"By the fruit of his lips will a man be satisfied"* (Proverbs 18:20). Your words will determine the course of your life. God already told you He's willing, so speak to your mountain. Remove the phrase "Lord willing" from your vocabulary unless it's to say, "Lord willing, next year, I'll preach in South Africa." Jesus could come back before you get the chance. But there's no "Lord willing" about your health, the multiplication of your ministry or business, and all the things God promised you. God already told you what He's willing to do. Open your Bible and find out for yourself.

Sometimes, when people hear teachings on confession, they conclude they need to guard what they say. It's a common response, especially within denominational churches. The pastor's wife might say, "I'm going to be careful what I say around you." Around me? God hears you all the time. This is not a doctrine invented by myself or Kenneth Hagin; this is Bible doctrine.

You can't even get saved until you believe in your heart and confess with your mouth. When you read about the power of your confession, it shouldn't trigger you to be careful of what you say. It should prompt you to open your mouth and declare, "These dry bones will live again," or "The property that the Lord laid on my heart for our church expansion, I call it ours."

Start talking like that. Put your words on it. In the Old Testament, they put their feet on it. In the New Testament, our words replace our feet. We put our words on the property that God said belongs to us in His Word. We don't march on it, we put our words on it. "I claim that in Jesus' name. I take that as mine. I take delivery of what God said belongs to me." Speak it out of your mouth with violence.

> And in the morning, as they passed by, they saw the fig tree dried up from the roots. And Peter calling to remembrance saith unto him, Master, behold, the fig tree which thou cursedst is withered away. And Jesus answering saith unto them, Have faith in God.
>
> — MARK 11:20-22 (KJV)

When Jesus cursed the fig tree, it looked the same as before he spoke to it. It didn't die from the outside in, it died from the inside out. That's where people miss it. When they curse something, it doesn't show on the outside. It's cursed from the root. Jesus said, *"May no one ever eat fruit from you again"* (Mark 11:14). The tree appeared unchanged, but when they walked by the next day, Peter said, *"Look, Rabbi! The fig tree you cursed has withered and died!"*

> ...behold, the fig tree which thou cursedst is withered away. And Jesus answering saith unto them, Have faith in God. For verily I say unto you, That whosoever shall say unto this mountain, Be thou removed, and be thou cast into the sea;

and shall not doubt in his heart, but shall believe that those things which he saith shall come to pass; he shall have whatsoever he saith.

— MARK 11:21-23 (KJV)

In these verses, Jesus mentioned *what you believe* one time and *what you say* three times. You must believe what you say. If I said it, it's done because God gave me the power in my tongue. People often say things they don't believe, but God promises you will have whatsoever you say. Know this:

 You can have whatever you say.

Therefore I say unto you, What things soever ye desire when ye pray, believe that ye receive them, and ye shall have them.

— MARK 11:24 (KJV)

Don't just read it; say it!

- I'll never be sick again.
- I'll never be broke another day in my life.
- I am rich.
- I am healed.
- I am righteous.
- I am anointed.
- I can do all things through Christ who strengthens me!
- I'm the head and not the tail.

I thank God I have parents who spoke life into my future and told me things like, "One day, you're going to be a great man of God." Those were the first words my dad spoke to me as a baby. It's not just about you, this world needs a new generation of children to grow up in homes with mothers and fathers who bless them—parents who are committed to doing what the Bible says in Proverbs 6:20-22 (NKJV). "*My son, keep your father's command, And do not forsake the law of your mother. Bind them contin-*

ually upon your heart; When you roam, they will lead you; When you sleep, they will keep you; And when you awake, they will speak with you." Tell your children they will be blessed, and they will be a blessing to their generation.

Decide to use your words to create life. Curse things that are of the Devil and speak the things that are of God. Whatever has set up shop in your life that's not of God, speak to it right now and curse it from the root—command it to die. You can command cancer to die. Jesus spoke to the fever and rebuked it. Quit asking people for prayer. Open your mouth and curse things sent by the Devil.

If you've never given your life to Jesus Christ, none of this will work for you. You can't exercise faith until faith comes alive. Once you put your faith in Jesus Christ, connect it to God.

CHAPTER 12

FASTING & PRAYER

Fasting is not punishment. Fasting is not a spiritual discipline. Fasting and prayer is a weapon of warfare that will loose every bond of wickedness that's tried to clamp down on you. I fast to loose the bonds of wickedness and to destroy oppression.

> When they returned to the other disciples, they saw a large crowd surrounding them, and some teachers of religious law were arguing with them. When the crowd saw Jesus, they were overwhelmed with awe, and they ran to greet him. "What is all this arguing about?" Jesus asked. One of the men in the crowd spoke up and said, "Teacher, I brought my son so you could heal him. He is possessed by an evil spirit that won't let him talk. And whenever this spirit seizes him, it throws him violently to the ground. Then he foams at the mouth and grinds his teeth and becomes rigid. So I asked your disciples to cast out the evil spirit, but they couldn't do it." Jesus said to them, "You faithless people! How long must I be with you? How long must I put up with you? Bring the boy to me." So they brought the boy. But when the evil spirit saw Jesus, it threw the child into a violent convulsion, and he

fell to the ground, writhing and foaming at the mouth. "How long has this been happening?" Jesus asked the boy's father. He replied, "Since he was a little boy. The spirit often throws him into the fire or into water, trying to kill him. Have mercy on us and help us, if you can." "What do you mean, 'If I can'?" Jesus asked. "Anything is possible if a person believes." The father instantly cried out, "I do believe, but help me overcome my unbelief!" When Jesus saw that the crowd of onlookers was growing, he rebuked the evil spirit. "Listen, you spirit that makes this boy unable to hear and speak," he said. "I command you to come out of this child and never enter him again!" Then the spirit screamed and threw the boy into another violent convulsion and left him. The boy appeared to be dead. A murmur ran through the crowd as people said, "He's dead." But Jesus took him by the hand and helped him to his feet, and he stood up. Afterward, when Jesus was alone in the house with his disciples, they asked him, "Why couldn't we cast out that evil spirit?" Jesus replied, "This kind can be cast out only by prayer and fasting."

— MARK 9:14-29

After returning from a time of prayer, Jesus still had to use His words to take authority. Words are the main channel to release God's power, but certain demonic powers won't come out without prayer and fasting. It's possible to reach a level that you can't break past. You can face a problem that you won't receive an answer to without engaging the weapon of fasting and prayer. Engaging this weapon can cause struggles you've battled for many years to be solved within three days. I formally invite you to participate in the 21-day fast with us at Revival Today Church at the beginning of every year.

Our crusade in Newark, New Jersey, was a product of fasting and prayer. There's a demonic resistance to crusade evangelism, but you can beat it with fasting and prayer. The Bible says, *"Then will your light break forth like the morning, your healing shall spring forth speedily"* (Isaiah 54:8).

Fasting and prayer causes your light to break out, and light drives out darkness. We have this treasure hidden in earthen vessels, but fasting and prayer takes the light out of hiding, breaks the earthen vessel, and allows the light to shine through, causing the darkness to flee. Engaging in fasting and prayer destroys every force of the Devil against your life.

Some may ask, "Wasn't Jesus speaking of the demon of unbelief in Mark 9?" It was not the demon of their unbelief. A demon made the boy deaf and mute, and the disciples couldn't cast it out. It was a literal demon that made the boy suffer a seizure. Listen to what Jesus said. He didn't say, "You demon of unbelief." He said, *"You spirit that makes this boy deaf and mute, I command you to come out of him and never enter him again."* When Jesus said those words, He stated, once and for all, that prayer will be answered regardless of who or what it is, in the presence of unwavering faith. All things will be given that are promised and provided by God in the Gospel.[i]

Jesus' answer to why the demon didn't depart is always correct for questions like this. All things that are promised and provided for by God in the Gospel will be given. All things that are promised in the Gospel pertain to life and godliness. Instead of accepting this, many modern followers have manufactured innumerable excuses for their lack of power. They offer conjecture claiming it may not be God's will, you may be under the chastening of God, the power to heal was for the apostles only, signs, gifts, and miracles ceased with the apostles, you may become prideful if God heard your prayers, healing is not in the atonement, or healing is not for today. None of these are true. They're just excuses for a lack of power. Maybe you've been around churches that lack power. They can't get anyone healed, so they make an excuse for it.[ii]

I once prayed for a man in a motorized wheelchair. I didn't ask, but he looked paralyzed from the neck down. When I prayed for him, he didn't walk, but he wheeled over to me in the parking lot and said, "Since you prayed for me, I can feel my arms and legs now. I can move them." That's a start. But I didn't say, "Well, he didn't get healed. I guess God wants him in the chair." No, I had to grow in the strength of the anointing to deliver people in need of a restorative miracle. If I can't reach my goal, it's not on God; it's on me. It won't push me to say,

"Well, I guess it doesn't always work." No, it causes me to press in even more. I will continue to press in stronger to carry the power of God to my generation.

Don't make excuses for a lack of power. First, understand Christ is your power source. Secondly, learn how to release His power based on the Word of God. It doesn't do anyone any good to know God has power and not know how to release it.

> Then he said, "Don't be afraid, Daniel. Since the first day you began to pray for understanding and to humble yourself before your God, your request has been heard in heaven. I have come in answer to your prayer. But for twenty-one days the spirit prince of the kingdom of Persia blocked my way. Then Michael, one of the archangels, came to help me, and I left him there with the spirit prince of the kingdom of Persia. Now I am here to explain what will happen to your people in the future, for this vision concerns a time yet to come."
>
> — DANIEL 10:12-14

Notice what the angel said: *"The first day you asked, your answer was sent."* Fasting isn't a method to persuade God to intervene; God answered Daniel immediately. For twenty-one days, a literal demon spirit kept the angel from bringing his answer, but as Daniel persisted in fasting and prayer, more angelic help was released. Fasting and prayer invokes angelic assistance on your behalf. Daniel's prayer and fasting provoked an archangel to attend to the problem he was facing. When Archangel Michael dealt with that demon, it freed up the first angel to deliver Daniel's answer. It's like football: Angel number one was struggling, so he caught a block from Angel number two and delivered the football to Daniel.

Fasting and prayer is a weapon to defeat the enemy. There are spiritual forces aligned against our advancement. Jesus said, *"I will build My church, and the gates of hell shall not prevail against it"* (Matthew 16:18), which means the very gates of Hell are aligned against the advancement of The Church. Our battle is not physical, it's spiritual. You must engage the spiritual power of fasting and prayer to destroy the things sent to destroy you.

I'm one of the few people you'll ever hear acknowledge demonic power and remain joyful. Be like me because it seems like there are two groups in the body of Christ. One group ignores demonic power, and the other group talks about demons nonstop. God gave us a weapon that swallows up evil—our rod swallows up all the other snakes. Say this:

 My rod swallows up all the other snakes.

God gave us ways to release the power He has given us. Jesus is the rod that proceeds out of the stem of Jesse. Fasting and prayer is not a religious discipline, it's a weapon. It's how we release the power that God gave us. People battle things for thirty years that could have been knocked out in three days of fasting and prayer. Not just fasting—fasting with prayer.

When you're facing a problem you don't understand, pray in the language you don't understand. *Pray always in the Holy Ghost, building up your most precious faith* (Jude 1:20). If you're not baptized in the Holy Ghost yet, get baptized in the Holy Ghost. If you've been going to a church for a decade and haven't received the baptism of the Holy Ghost, there is a good chance you're in a lousy church. You shouldn't have to go to a youth camp or retreat to receive the baptism of the Holy Ghost. You should go to a church where it's difficult to be in a service without being filled with the Holy Ghost.

CHAPTER 13

TOUCH

Another way to release God's power is through touch. The Bible says, *"You will lay your hands on the sick, and the sick will recover"* (Mark 16:18). When cloth or aprons were taken from Paul and laid on the sick, people were healed from any sickness or disease, and any demon spirit came out. That's the power of touch.

The laying on of hands, anointing cloth, and anointing with oil are the three points of contact. *"Wherever your foot shall tread, you will be on land that I have given to you"* (Joshua 1:3). So put your feet on the ground.

When we held our first crusade in Philadelphia, I went to the field every night and walked the entirety of the property as I drizzled it with olive oil at about one in the morning. I committed that ground to the Lord—and we still do that. It changes things.

A lady in Newark commented, "As soon as I came on the ground, I felt like I didn't have to stay in my wheelchair. I could feel my feet, and I got up and walked out of my wheelchair with no prayer." That's why we put our feet on the ground. Confront the problem.

If you're a pastor who can't get a building permit, go to the office and speak with force. Don't deal with things from far away. David didn't pray about Goliath or curse Goliath from Jesse's house, David put his feet on the ground, faced Goliath, and went at him. What you don't confront, you'll never conquer. Whatever you don't resist has the right to remain. If you're believing for property, put your feet on the property you desire to obtain. March around it. Thank God in advance as you march. "Thank you, Father, that wherever I put my feet, I'll be on land that You've given me." Put action to your faith.

Lay hands on the sick. If you have a child who's having trouble, put their head in your hands and pray for any drug or alcohol addiction to be broken in the name of Jesus. You'll always feel resistance when you do something like that because when a barrier is broken, it brings victory.

Smith Wigglesworth told a story about a time when preachers stayed in homes before hotels and motels were common. As he was leaving a home he'd stayed in, the lady of the house began crying and said, "You can't leave yet, Brother Wigglesworth. My husband is unsaved. He's on his way to Hell. I prayed and fasted that he would get saved this week, and he never came to one of your meetings. He's still unsaved. Please stay."

He told the lady he had to go but instructed her not to change the sheets on the bed. He had stayed in the master bedroom during his visit. When the couple moved back into the master bedroom, she left the sheets unchanged. On the first night, while they were sleeping, the husband began to toss and turn and asked his wife if she was hot as well. Of course, it wasn't hot in there. They were in England where it's never hot.

He continued thrashing until finally he got up, knelt down beside the bed, and cried his eyes out, saying, "Forgive me a sinner, Oh Lord. Forgive me a sinner. I'm so convicted." The anointing on Wigglesworth was transferred to those sheets just like it transferred to Paul's garments.

If my child were away from God, I'd lay in their bed and pray in the Holy Ghost. Put action to your faith. What action specifically? Put your feet down. Put your hands on it. Put some cloth on it. Put some anointing oil on it. It consecrates anything it touches. It may leave the factory an ordinary product, but when you bless it, it carries the actual power of the Holy Ghost. Put it on your children, use it when sickness tries to attack. These are the ways God gives us to release His power. That rod swallows up all the serpents. There's no case too tough for God.

"Rule now in the midst of your enemies" (Psalm 110:2). God's power overwhelms everything that's made itself an enemy of your marriage, your family, or your finances.

CHAPTER 14

PRAISE

One reason Christians stay in trouble is because when they're faced with a storm, they say things like, "Well, I'm just trusting Jesus." But that won't help get you out of the storm. You don't trust Jesus to get you out of your problems. You must be full of the Holy Ghost and know how to release the anointing and power of God. In the previous chapters, we discussed how to use your mouth, leverage the power of prayer and fasting, and harness the power of touch to release God's power. There's one final channel to release God's power in any situation.

> One day as we were going down to the place of prayer, we met a slave girl who had a spirit that enabled her to tell the future. She earned a lot of money for her masters by telling fortunes. She followed Paul and the rest of us, shouting, "These men are servants of the Most High God, and they have come to tell you how to be saved." This went on day after day until Paul got so exasperated that he turned and said to the demon within her, "I command you in the name of Jesus Christ to come out of her." And instantly it left her. Her masters' hopes of wealth were now shattered, so they grabbed Paul and Silas and dragged them before the authori-

ties at the marketplace. "The whole city is in an uproar because of these Jews!" they shouted to the city officials. "They are teaching customs that are illegal for us Romans to practice." A mob quickly formed against Paul and Silas, and the city officials ordered them stripped and beaten with wooden rods. They were severely beaten, and then they were thrown into prison. The jailer was ordered to make sure they didn't escape. So the jailer put them into the inner dungeon and clamped their feet in the stocks. Around midnight Paul and Silas were praying and singing hymns to God, and the other prisoners were listening. Suddenly, there was a massive earthquake, and the prison was shaken to its foundations. All the doors immediately flew open, and the chains of every prisoner fell off! The jailer woke up to see the prison doors wide open. He assumed the prisoners had escaped, so he drew his sword to kill himself. But Paul shouted to him, "Stop! Don't kill yourself! We are all here!" The jailer called for lights and ran to the dungeon and fell down trembling before Paul and Silas. Then he brought them out and asked, "Sirs, what must I do to be saved?" They replied, "Believe in the Lord Jesus and you will be saved, along with everyone in your household." And they shared the word of the Lord with him and with all who lived in his household. Even at that hour of the night, the jailer cared for them and washed their wounds. Then he and everyone in his household were immediately baptized. He brought them into his house and set a meal before them, and he and his entire household rejoiced because they all believed in God. The next morning the city officials sent the police to tell the jailer, "Let those men go!" So the jailer told Paul, "The city officials have said you and Silas are free to leave. Go in peace."

— ACTS 16:16-36

The same people who begged for Paul and Silas to be jailed ended up begging them to leave the jail and the city. The Bible says that Paul and

Silas prayed and sang praises unto God, and instantly there was a violent earthquake. The earthquake didn't happen after they prayed, it happened after they praised God.

THE POWER OF PRAISE

1. Praise ensures that you thank God properly for all that He's done.

The Bible says in Romans 1 that because they would not thank God or give Him praise, their minds became darkened and confused, and it led to demonic control. That's why we're commanded to be in church every Sunday. It's vital to take the first hours of every week and offer praise to God. If you skip over this command, you're in danger.

Deuteronomy 28:47-48 says, *"If you do not serve the Lord your God with joy and enthusiasm for the abundant benefits you have received, you will serve your enemies whom the Lord will send against you."* Praising God removes you from the company of the types of people mentioned in Romans 1 and Deuteronomy 28, who didn't praise God and opened themselves to demonic attack.

God counts it as a serious offense for you to find something else to do with your Sunday mornings after he sent His only begotten Son to die and showered you with great blessings. He takes praise so seriously that if you don't praise Him, even the rocks will cry out.

If you read a Presbyterian catechism book, the first question is: Why were you created? The answer is: To show forth praise unto God. That's my primary reason for existing. God can do everything, except thank and praise Himself. That's why the angels sing around the clock.

Separate yourself from people who are bitter or arrogant and don't return praise to God. Bitterness and arrogance are at the heart o why people don't return praise. You'd have to be arrogant to think you don't need to praise God or to think you can get away without honoring God in His house. That's true arrogance. The only other explanation is bitterness. Maybe the Devil convinced you to blame God, so you withhold your praise. But when you return praise unto God, you leave the category of people who irritate God and join the company of those who please God. Until you thank God for the last thing He's done, you're disqualified from receiving the next thing.

Before Jesus multiplied the loaves and fish, He thanked God for it. What kind of lunatic thanks God for five loaves and two fish when you have 15,000 to 20,000 people to feed? Most people would have said, "What am I supposed to do with this?" But Jesus said, *"Father, I thank You for this food,"* and after He gave thanks, it began to multiply. Likewise, when He stood at the tomb of Lazarus, before He called Lazarus out, He thanked God (John 11:41-42).

Most people rush into prayer with no thought or thankfulness, just empty words. It only takes a few seconds to say, "Father, I thank You that You always hear me. You've answered all my prayers." Jesus started by thanking and praising God. It's not just a religious exercise. Praise is a very powerful spiritual weapon that God has given us. Praise assures that you've thanked God properly. Once you thank God for what He's done, you've put yourself in a position to see multiplication and performance.

2. Praise produces joy.

The United States of America consumes more prescription drugs than any other country. We're not the largest country by population; we're not even close. How can people living here consume more prescription drugs than the rest of the world? It shouldn't surprise you to know the most prescribed drug classification is antidepressants. It surpassed heart medication as the most prescribed drug around 2015.[i] With symptoms of depression, fear, anxiety, and panic attacks as prevalent as they are, it's important to loose the weapon of praise because praise produces joy. You can't praise God and remain sad. That's why the Bible says in James 5:13, *"Are any of you merry, he should sing."*

In The Old Testament, you weren't allowed to serve in the temple if you were depressed. In the New Testament, if you're depressed, you're not allowed to sing. When you praise God, it produces joy. David encouraged himself in the Lord. Put on the garment of praise for the spirit of heaviness.

> But Thou art holy, O Thou that inhabitest the praises of Israel.
>
> — PSALM 22:3 (KJV)

God abides in the praises of His people. God's presence comes in when you praise Him. The Bible says, *"In His presence is the fullness of joy, at His right hand pleasure forevermore"* (Psalm 16:11). So, you can't be a person who praises and be depressed because the joy of the Lord is your strength. If praise produces joy, then praise strengthens the praiser enabling them to do what God has called them to do.

3. Praise creates an atmosphere in which Satan cannot operate.

God and the Devil will not cohabitate someday. They will never share the same space. When you offer praise, God steps in, and when He does, every devil and everything that's of the Devil must leave.

In old-time Pentecost, we used to bind the Devil every eight minutes, "Satan, we bind you, Satan." When I was ten years old, I started to think, 'If that sucker is so slippery that he gets loose every eight minutes, we're fighting a losing battle.' If you've ever been to one of my meetings, you've heard me instruct the congregation to repeat after me and say things like: "Hallelujah! Praise the Lord! The Lord is good, and His mercy endures forever!" I do that because it's a lot more effective than having people say, "Satan, we bind you." When you praise God, the Devil leaves on his own.

The first time I went to India, I preached on praise and instructed everybody to lift their hands and let out a shout of victory for one minute. As everyone began to shout, nine girls—some of whom were Hindu temple prostitutes—were thrown down to the ground and began to slither like snakes. The demon spirits within them left without anyone having to cast them out. I realized then that praise creates an atmosphere demons can't stay in.

When someone claims they have a demon in their house, it's almost never surprising, because it's a depressing atmosphere. There's no joy. There's a problem if there's no laughter in your house. *"A merry heart doeth good like a medicine, but a broken spirit drieth the bones"* (Proverbs 17:22). There's an atmosphere in which healing flows, and it's an atmosphere of praise and thanksgiving. It's not an atmosphere of concern. Whatever need you have, don't allow that need to dominate your psyche and personality. Learn how to lift holy hands unto God without wrath or doubting and begin to sing praises.

Paul was not in great circumstances when he was severely beaten and thrown in prison. But as soon as he had some time alone, he lifted his hands and began to sing and move. I can picture him wiggling his feet in the stocks. Praise isn't simply a vocal exercise, you're to move your body. Visit a church in Africa, and you'll see how they dance on their way into church, dance in church, and dance on their way out of church. If you grew up in North America, people shuffle in looking like the third guy from the left on the evolutionary chart, hunched over like someone put two hundred pounds around their neck. That's not how it's supposed to be. Psalm 100:4 says, *"I'll enter His gates with thanksgiving in my heart. I'll come into His courts with praise."*

Take time to praise God today, and it'll literally drive the Devil out of your affairs and out of your presence. You don't have to bind the Devil, just praise God.

4. Praise provokes God's delivering power.

The Bible doesn't say the apostles prayed, and an earthquake came. It says they prayed, but nothing happened. Then they sang praises unto God, and that's when the earthquake came.

Visualize two scales, like the scales of justice. One scale is marked *prayer*, and the other is marked *praise*. For many people, prayer would be weighted to the bottom, and praise would be empty. But if you balance it out and let your praise catch up with your prayer, you'll experience an earthquake. Praise provokes God's delivering power.

In Daniel 10, a demon spirit held up Daniel's answer for twenty-one days. A demon spirit has the power to contend with an angel, but nothing has the power to contend with God. The Bible says God Himself abides in the praises of His people. When God steps in, no demon can stop Him. Satan himself can't hold Him up. That's why praise is called the highest form of prayer.

The more knowledge you gain from the Word of God, the less you'll ask for things. You'll simply start praising God, because you'll know it's already yours according to the Word. You'll know it's done. Begin to thank God that His Word is true and give Him praise for it ahead of time.

When Jericho's walls fell flat, they didn't shout after they fell; they shouted to provoke them to crumble. The shout of the Lord leveled the walls of Jericho. Paul didn't praise God after he broke out of prison. He praised God while in jail, and his praise broke him out. We're a peculiar people. We don't wait till the battle is over; we shout ahead of time without even having to fight. If praise could knock iron chains off from Paul and Silas' wrists, break the stocks off their feet, and open all the prison doors, how much more can it demolish the invisible bands that are around you?

When you praise God, everything that's binding you, everything that represents a prison, and everything that's thwarting your progress, falls off immediately in the name of Jesus Christ.

5. Praise keeps you from becoming a permanent prayer project.

If you don't do what Paul and Silas did, if you just pray and don't praise God, then you always carry the weight of what you're praying for. Some people never break free because they continue praying until they get a modicum of victory, then they praise God.

When you praise, you're calling it done. You're celebrating the victory. As you praise the Lord, your victory is finalized. Pray once and then give God the praise, and you'll experience the same power that was at work in Acts 16 take effect in your life. Praise God for it. Give God the glory. Call it done—over. You're delivered. God heard your prayer. He's done it. What a mighty God. Start praising God. Pray one time and believe for it to be done. Jesus never kept anyone in prayer.

Not everyone can praise God. Only those who are His children can praise Him. If you've never given your life to Jesus Christ, you can't use this weapon. Whoever is born of God overcomes the world, and this is the victory that overcomes the world, even our faith. Until God's seed is in you, until you're born again, you don't have access to release His power because His power is not in you.

PART IV
FINAL LESSONS

CHAPTER 15

13 LESSONS FROM THE BOOK OF JOB

Life has battles you must fight, or you're at risk of the default—defeat. The default is children who don't serve the Lord, bankruptcy, lack, frustration, sickness, depression, and death. You don't have to do anything to get those things, but you must fight the good fight of faith to lay hold of that which Christ Jesus has promised you. The Bible doesn't say Jesus came so that you would have depression and children who don't serve the Lord. The Bible says Jesus came to give you abundant life.

I can't teach you how to prevail in every battle of life without discussing everyone's favorite temporarily defeated Bible character. After preaching about the redemptive power of Jesus and the Pauline revelation of being in Christ for three hours, someone inevitably always says, "Yeah, but what about Job?"

In this chapter, I will provide thirteen lessons from the Book of Job. I'll discuss what you can take away from Job's book.

Did God really write a bunch of victory verses like:

> *you can prevail in every battle of life…*
> *no weapon formed against you will prosper…*
> *every tongue that rises against you shall be condemned…*
> *when your enemy attacks you from one direction, I'll make him run from you in seven directions?*

Did He then throw one book in the Bible that counteracts what He said in the other sixty-five books? More likely, people have been poorly interpreting the Book of Job. Obviously, God doesn't say two different things. He doesn't have a forked tongue. The Bible says God doesn't contradict Himself. The Bible says one consistent thing. Anytime you hear someone say, "I know God said that, but He also said…." Remember, God has never and will never say two different things. The issue lies in the understanding of what God said.

The Bible is consistent. God is a Healer from the beginning of the Bible to the end of the Bible. He's a Savior from the beginning of the Bible to the end of the Bible. He's not evil in the beginning. He's not evil in the middle. He's not evil in the end. He didn't come to bring death and destruction to people. He came to bring life.

> There once was a man named Job who lived in the land of Uz. He was blameless—a man of complete integrity. He feared God and stayed away from evil. He had seven sons and three daughters. He owned 7,000 sheep, 3,000 camels, 500 teams of oxen, and 500 female donkeys. He also had many servants. He was, in fact, the richest person in that entire area. Job's sons would take turns preparing feasts in their homes, and they would also invite their three sisters to celebrate with them. When these celebrations ended—sometimes after several days—Job would purify his children. He would get up early in the morning and offer a burnt offering for each of them. For Job said to himself, "Perhaps my children have sinned and have cursed God in their hearts." This was Job's regular practice. One day the members of the

heavenly court came to present themselves before the Lord, and the Accuser, Satan, came with them. "Where have you come from?" the Lord asked Satan. Satan answered the Lord, "I have been patrolling the earth, watching everything that's going on." Then the Lord asked Satan, "Have you noticed my servant Job? He is the finest man in all the earth. He is blameless—a man of complete integrity. He fears God and stays away from evil." Satan replied to the Lord, "Yes, but Job has good reason to fear God. You have always put a wall of protection around him and his home and his property. You have made him prosper in everything he does. Look how rich he is! But reach out and take away everything he has, and he will surely curse you to your face!" "All right, you may test him," the Lord said to Satan. "Do whatever you want with everything he possesses, but don't harm him physically." So Satan left the Lord's presence. One day when Job's sons and daughters were feasting at the oldest brother's house, a messenger arrived at Job's home with this news: "Your oxen were plowing, with the donkeys feeding beside them, when the Sabeans raided us. They stole all the animals and killed all the farmhands. I am the only one who escaped to tell you." While he was still speaking, another messenger arrived with this news: "The fire of God has fallen from heaven and burned up your sheep and all the shepherds. I am the only one who escaped to tell you." While he was still speaking, a third messenger arrived with this news: "Three bands of Chaldean raiders have stolen your camels and killed your servants. I am the only one who escaped to tell you." While he was still speaking, another messenger arrived with this news: "Your sons and daughters were feasting in their oldest brother's home. Suddenly, a powerful wind swept in from the wilderness and hit the house on all sides. The house collapsed, and all your children are dead. I am the only one who escaped to tell you." Job stood up and tore his robe in grief. Then he shaved his head and fell to the ground to worship. He said, "I came naked from my mother's womb, and I will be naked when I leave. The Lord gave me what I had, and the Lord has taken it away. Praise the name of the Lord!" In all of this, Job did not sin by blaming God.

— JOB 1:1-22

One day the members of the heavenly court came again to present themselves before the Lord, and the Accuser, Satan, came with them. "Where have you come from?" the Lord asked Satan. Satan answered the Lord, "I have been patrolling the earth, watching everything that's going on." Then the Lord asked Satan, "Have you noticed my servant Job? He is the finest man in all the earth. He is blameless—a man of complete integrity. He fears God and stays away from evil. And he has maintained his integrity, even though you urged me to harm him without cause." Satan replied to the Lord, "Skin for skin! A man will give up everything he has to save his life. But reach out and take away his health, and he will surely curse you to your face!" "All right, do with him as you please," the Lord said to Satan. "But spare his life." So Satan left the Lord's presence, and he struck Job with terrible boils from head to foot. Job scraped his skin with a piece of broken pottery as he sat among the ashes. His wife said to him, "Are you still trying to maintain your integrity? Curse God and die."But Job replied, "You talk like a foolish woman. Should we accept only good things from the hand of God and never anything bad?" So in all this, Job said nothing wrong.

— JOB 2:1-10

Let's get into the thirteen lessons you can learn from the Book of Job. After you finish reading these thirteen lessons, the Devil will never again be able to use the Book of Job as a caveat to the precious promises of God that belong to you.

1. You Can Please God

One of the things I love most about reading those first two chapters in Job is that God is up in Heaven bragging about Job. God didn't call Job a scoundrel and complain about how His servant irritated and disobeyed Him all the time. He said, "Have you noticed My servant, Job? He's perfect in all his ways. He wants nothing to do with evil and loves what is good. He serves Me. He fears Me."

Job pleased God two covenants ago. He lived before the law and the Levitical covenant through Moses. Hebrews 8:6 says, *"For he is the one who mediates for us a far better covenant with God, based on better promises."* Job lived before the covenant that was deemed worse than the one we're under now. If Job could gain the approval of God two covenants ago, don't ever think you can't please God under your current covenant.

Religious churches teach people to think God sees them as a bother and that He's angry with everyone, but you can live in the will of God and please Him. You can live your life in such a way that God speaks about you the way He spoke about Job: "Have you noticed Jonathan? I'm proud of him. Did you see that he had an opportunity to sin and didn't do it?" Think about that. You can live life in a manner that God sits in Heaven not upset with you but well-pleased.

When Jesus says, *"Well done, My good and faithful servant,"* it won't be the first time He's ever felt that way about you. He's felt that way toward you the entire time He's been watching you live your righteous life. When He gets the chance to tell you in person, He'll recount all the times you had the opportunity to turn back, yet you stayed the course. He knows all the times you didn't go the way everyone else went. He saw when you faced opposition but pressed on in faith. He's pleased that you never gave up and quit.

2. Satan Was the One Who Took

Satan is a taker. The Bible tells us, *"The thief cometh not, but for to steal, and to kill, and to destroy"* (John 10:10).

When Job said, *"Should we accept the good things that come from the hand of God and never the bad?"* Job was wrong to say it. If you continue reading, Job went on to say, *"Forgive me. I was talking about things I know nothing about"* (Job 42:3).

God rebuked Job for a chapter and a half for suggesting He was the cause of the bad things Job endured, but Job didn't have a Bible and he didn't know anything about the Devil. There was no need for Job to know anything about the Devil because even if he knew the Devil was the cause of his suffering, he didn't have the authority to do anything about it. The story of Job allows us to realize the power that comes with our new covenant with Jesus Christ. Jesus hadn't yet been born to tell Job, *"Behold, I give you authority over all the power of the Devil"* (Luke 10:19). So, he had zero authority over the enemy.

No one ever cast out a devil in the Old Testament. Not Elijah, Elisha, or Moses. After Adam sinned, Satan had full control of the Earth. Jesus was born a man to take it back. Before then, no one had the power to dominate the Devil with their words like we can now. No one could cast out devils. That's why when Jesus cast out devils, the people marveled and said, *"What is this? What new doctrine is this? For with authority He commands even the unclean spirits, and they obey Him"* (Mark 1:27). Then Jesus said in Luke 11:20, *"But if I with the finger of God cast out devils, no doubt the kingdom of God is come upon you."* Jesus left people in awe, *"When Jesus had ended these sayings, that the people were astonished at His teaching, for He taught them as one having authority, and not as the scribes"* (Matthew 7:28-29). They reacted this way because Jesus had done something never done before under the old covenant.

Satan is the one who takes. Don't get confused by the verses that resulted in Job's rebuke. "Well, the Lord gives and the Lord takes away." No. God didn't agree with that, and neither should you.

There is a song that has been like a thorn in my flesh for many years. The lyrics say, "He gives and takes away. But my heart will choose to say, blessed be the name." That's not the new covenant.

I once preached for an old Pentecostal preacher. During worship and praise, he was focused on reviewing the order of the service with his glasses low on his nose and wasn't paying attention to the music. As they began to sing that song, his head snapped up, and he asked, "What are they singing?"

"They're singing 'He gives and takes away,'" I replied

"Job said that, and he was wrong."

"I know, but they're your worship team," I responded.

After service, he rebuked the worship team and told them to never sing that song again because it's unscriptural.

When bad things try to invade your life, you don't sit idly by with no response. That's not New Testament Christianity. You must understand the Bible in context. If you believe God takes away your blessings, then you should also start sacrificing bulls and goats and travel to the Wailing Wall to pray. Stop using the name of Jesus when you pray. Instead, visit a high priest, tell him your sin, have him lay hands on a goat once a year, and walk it out to the middle of the desert to die in your place.

We're not under the old covenant. Jesus fulfilled the old covenant, which Job predates. Jesus fulfilled the old covenant and brought us into a new covenant. Satan was the one who created sickness and brought disease. Satan was the one who destroyed the family. Satan was the one who brought wickedness into the world.

> Every good gift and every perfect gift is from above, and cometh down from the Father of lights, with Whom is no variableness, neither shadow of turning.
>
> — JAMES 1:17 (KJV)

3. God Was the One Who Gave

God gave Job everything he had. *"Have you considered My servant Job, that there is none like him on the earth, a blameless and upright man, one who fears God and shuns evil?"* (Job 1:8). Even the Devil had to testify that God abundantly blessed Job, *"Have You not made a hedge around him, around his house-*

hold, and around all that he has on every side? You have blessed the work of his hands, and his possessions have increased in the land" (Job 1:10). Riches don't come from the Devil. When the Devil came on the scene, he didn't bring riches. He arrived with the sole intent to destroy everything. If money is of the Devil, why did Satan desire to take all of Job's money? It was because God had blessed him with it. *"The thief comes to steal, kill, and destroy. I have come that you might have life and have it more abundantly"* (John 10:10).

When Scripture says, *"In all these things, Job said nothing wrong,"* there are two things you must understand. First, it refers to Job's limited knowledge. He didn't say anything wrong as far as he *knew*. Secondly, it means he didn't say anything wrong in blaming God. He didn't speak *against* God; he spoke incorrectly *about* God out of ignorance. He didn't talk like his wife and say, *"Curse God and die."* He refused to speak against God. So, in his ignorance, he didn't sin.

The Bible is filled with verses that speak to God's giving and compassionate nature.

> God so loved the world that He **gave**.
>
> — JOHN 3:16

> Every good and perfect gift is from above, and comes down from the Father of lights, with whom there is no variation or shadow of turning.
>
> — JAMES 1:17 (NKJV)

> He who did not spare His own Son, but delivered Him up for us all, how shall He not with Him also freely **give** us all things?
>
> — ROMANS 8:32 (NKJV)

> **Give**, and it will be given to you.
>
> — LUKE 6:38

> Do not withhold good from those to whom it is due, when it is in the power of your hand to do so.
>
> — PROVERBS 3:27 (NKJV)

God is a giver, and He put His nature in us. Satan is a taker. God gave Job every good thing he received, and Satan took every good thing Job lost. Don't get it confused. It's not the Lord gave, and the Lord took. You may have heard some backslidden preachers say that at a five-year-old's funeral, "Well, God needed another flower for His garden." It's no surprise if all eighty family members have no desire to attend church anymore. Who would want to serve a God who rips a young child from his family? It's a lie!

God clearly says, *"With long life will I satisfy you"* (Psalm 91:16). God is not the author of tragedy. He doesn't send tornadoes to blow through trailer parks. People who refer to natural disasters as "acts of God" are deceived. Do you really believe God is in Heaven rolling dice to decide which trailer park in Kansas He's going to wipe out? I don't think so. It's not in the Bible. Satan is the taker. God is the giver of every good and perfect gift. Know this truth:

 God is the giver of every good and perfect gift.

God doesn't give and take. He gives and gives some more. God will remove sin and other negative things from your life, but He doesn't take your children's lives. He didn't kill Job's livestock. He's not a destroyer. He's an increaser.

4. Job Helps You Understand Your Covenant

> But now Jesus, our High Priest, has been given a ministry that is far superior to the old priesthood, for he is the one who mediates for us a far better covenant with God, based on better promises.
>
> — HEBREWS 8:6

Job's story helps you better appreciate the covenant you have with God. Your covenant with God is based on better promises that Job didn't have access to. But does the thought remain that if Satan wanted to, he could meet with God, make an arrangement to violate the hedge of protection around your life, and take everything? Let me explain why a New Testament believer could never experience what Job endured.

Satan was able to gain access to Job because his righteousness was based on his justification. Satan insisted that if he was allowed to touch all that belonged to Job, he would surely curse God. Since Jesus hadn't come yet, Job could only be justified by his works. He had to prove his justification to God, but we are not justified by works, we're justified by faith in Jesus Christ. Satan cannot gain access to any New Testament believer by calling our works into question as he did with Job.

Not only can Satan not access us based on our works, he can no longer access God to call our works into question. He can no longer go to Heaven. Satan was able to discuss Job with God because he went to make war in Heaven, but the Bible says he prevailed not and was cast down (Revelation 12:7-9).

Even if Satan found a way to weasel his way back to Heaven and decided to petition God and say, "Look how you've blessed Jonathan, but let me touch Adalis and Camila, and I can get him to curse You to Your face." God would say something to the effect of, "You're too late. He's not earning his justification with Me through works. Jonathan's faith in Christ's obedience gives him justification with Me." A New Testament believer can never be attacked the way Job was attacked because the blood of Jesus ratified our covenant.

5. Job's Entire Ordeal Lasted Eighteen Months

According to Bible scholars, Job lived for an additional 140 years after his attack ended. When people claim to be like Job because they've been struggling for thirty-one years, there's a lack of understanding. Job's struggle only lasted a year and a half. Job is not the poster boy for prolonged suffering. Two covenants before Jesus was born, Job found a way to end his struggles by the power of God in prayer after eighteen months. How can anyone use Job as an excuse for prolonged suffering? Job's whole ordeal lasted less than the span of toddlerhood. For the New Testament believer, even eighteen months is too long—none of this applies. Paul called it our "momentary light affliction," nothing can scripturally go beyond momentary or light.

When I held a crusade in Asbury Park, five hundred people protested against it and made threats, but no one touched me. Their biggest tactical strategy was to blow bubbles while I preached. I've preached in locations where machine guns were being fired. Reminding me of times spent with my daughter in my front yard is not concerning. Momentary and light, to say the least.

6. No Jesus = No Authority

This may be the most important key: Job didn't have Jesus. Jesus' absence reveals the weakness of Job's covenant and the strength of our own.

> "God is not a mortal like me, so I cannot argue with him or take him to trial. If only there were a mediator between us, someone who could bring us together. The mediator could make God stop beating me, and I would no longer live in terror of his punishment. Then I could speak to him without fear, but I cannot do that in my own strength."
>
> — JOB 9:32-35

"If only there was a Mediator between us, Someone who could bring us together." The Hebrew word picture for what Job is describing is an *umpire*. "If only there was Someone to stand between me and God. Someone who could put one hand on my shoulder and one on God's shoulder and bring us together." Job didn't have that, but Jesus is our Mediator and High Priest who goes to God on our behalf. Job was crying out to God, asking for Him to send His Son, and without knowing it, he was saying, "I wish I had Jesus." Job couldn't say, "Father, in Jesus' name." The veil in the Temple hadn't been ripped yet. The Temple wasn't even built yet.

Pre-Jesus people in the Bible wanted what we have now: To appear boldly before the throne, make their request known, and then stamp it with "in Jesus' name," and it is done. Abraham, Job, and Elijah didn't have it, but look what they were still able to accomplish. Now, we have a better covenant built on better promises. You realize the weakness of their covenant when you see the strength of ours.

> "But as for me, I know that my Redeemer lives, and he will stand upon the earth at last."
>
> — JOB 19:25

Job began to prophesy in verse 25. He knew the One who would make his desire possible was alive, but not yet on Earth.

The Book of Job was written to help you appreciate what Jesus did for you. Christ came to fill the gaping hole Satan could access to attack man. Christ did away with it. Job didn't have Christ, but we have Him. So, the New Testament believer has no excuse for defeat.

7. Satan Attacked Job's Family

Satan's goal is to destroy the family. You can trust in God to keep your family secure. It doesn't matter if Satan aims is to destroy it, God's will is for your family to be whole.

8. Satan Took Job's Joy

Job went from being rich and enjoying his family to sitting in ashes and scraping his skin with pottery as he moaned and bled. Satan took Job from happiness to sorrow. Satan goes after your joy because the joy of the Lord is your strength.

9. Satan Went after Job's Money

Satan didn't just decimate Job's family; he took away all his sheep, livestock, and everything the Lord had given him. Satan will attack your assets. When you experience an attack on your assets, it's not God; it's Satan.

10. Satan Attacked Job's Body

Satan wanted Job's body. Sickness is from the Devil. The Bible says in Job 2:7, *"Then Satan went forth from the presence of God and smote Job with boils."* The Bible also says in the New Testament that Michael argued with Satan over Moses' body. Because Satan could never get to Moses' body when he was alive, he wanted to destroy his body after he died.

Satan hates your human body. He wants to see teenagers cut themselves. He likes to see people stricken with anorexia, bulimia, heroin addiction, strokes, paralysis, and the like. He enjoys it when our bodies suffer because we were created in the image of God. Satan can't afflict God, so he comes after us and does everything he can to destroy our bodies. Why do you think Jesus spent so much of His time restoring people? Satan hates your body, but God has a will to protect your body.

11. Satan Breached the Hedge of Protection Around Job

We've already established that the hedge of protection is intact for the New Testament believer, and we discovered how Satan breached it. The means he used to breach it can never be used against the New Testament believer.

There is a hedge around us. God doesn't just protect and bless you; He protects the blessed *and* protects their blessing. If Satan desires to steal, kill, and destroy, why isn't everyone stolen from, killed, and destroyed? He can't take out whomever he wants. *"He goes about like a roaring lion seeking whom he may devour"* (1 Peter 5:8). He can't devour everybody, and he sure can't devour me. He can't devour you if the blood of Christ covers you. Once you've been redeemed by the Blood, there's a hedge of protection around you, plus angels. *"For he will order his angels to protect you wherever you go"* (Psalm 91:11). In 2 Kings 19, one angel killed 185,000 enemy soldiers in one night. You are thoroughly protected.

You can breach your hedge of protection by stepping outside of it. Without God's protection, Satan will wipe you out. But if you stay in your covenant with God, you're within an unreachable, impenetrable hedge of protection. It's around you, your family, and everything you own.

12. Satan Is Arrogant

Satan wants to get you to curse God. He's looking for every opportunity to frustrate, confuse, and attack you until you mock God. The Devil is such an arrogant punk.

If I backslid and left my wife and daughter, picked up a cocaine habit, and moved in with my girlfriend, many others would backslide too. They'd start to think everything I had been preaching was all fake.

No major news station covers our ministry when we hold crusades, but if I were charged with one crime, the headline would read, "National evangelist busted by police."

Determine today to love the Lord with all your heart, soul, and physical strength, and never turn back. Make this declaration:

 I will never give the Devil the satisfaction of saying, "I got you to curse God."

13. Read to the End

The Book of Job ends with chapter 42.

> When Job prayed for his friends, the Lord restored his fortunes. In fact, the Lord gave him twice as much as before! Then all his brothers, sisters, and former friends came and feasted with him in his home. And they consoled him and comforted him because of all the trials the Lord had brought against him. And each of them brought him a gift of money and a gold ring. So the Lord blessed Job in the second half of his life even more than in the beginning. For now he had 14,000

> sheep, 6,000 camels, 1,000 teams of oxen, and 1,000 female donkeys. He also gave Job seven more sons and three more daughters. He named his first daughter Jemimah, the second Keziah, and the third Keren-happuch. In all the land no women were as lovely as the daughters of Job. And their father put them into his will along with their brothers. Job lived 140 years after that, living to see four generations of his children and grandchildren. Then he died, an old man who had lived a long, full life.
>
> — JOB 42:10-17

What do you do when you've been attacked? Perhaps you've lost a spouse, a child, a business, or someone or something dear to you. The lesson from the Book of Job is to believe God for double after you've suffered an attack. The God of restoration will make the Devil give back double what was taken from you. The story doesn't end with, "Job survived." The story concludes with Job experiencing greater blessings in the second half of his life than in the first half.

Whatever attack comes to your life, whatever's gone wrong up until now, you can pray to God. He will not only lift you out of the pit, He'll stand you up on the rock and increase you. The latter half of your life will be the greatest half. You and God can write a final chapter to your story that cancels all the previous chapters.

Stop dwelling on the attack. Instead, hook up with God and make the Devil pay for what he did. That's the message of the Book of Job. It doesn't end with him bleeding and dying. It ends with him old and rich, with children and grandchildren. He lived 140 years after his attack. Do you think he was still troubled by those eighteen months 110 years later? If you had something happen to you in 1914, would you be talking about it right now? God can overwhelm your greatest pain with His supernatural blessing, so you don't even remember the pain anymore. Hallelujah! Praise God!

Early in my ministry, I preached at a church in New England. We only had one hundred dollars in the bank at the time. We had the option to stay in a decent hotel that would leave us with twenty dollars in the bank, or we could rough it out in a cheap motel to save money. We opted to take our chances with the motel, and it turned out to be a dump that allowed pets. We could see the fleas on the bed when it was time to go to sleep. I remember telling my wife, "It won't always be like this. This is the lowest we'll ever be. God will take us up from here." I could see the look of concern on her face. We hadn't been married long, and I didn't want to lose her.

Those days are gone forever. The days of needing this week's offering to pay last week's bills have been gone for a long time. Now, all we see is continual victory in the form of million-dollar offering after million-dollar offering, in the form of land acquisition, and property, in the form of a private jet and fuel to fill it, in the form of breakthroughs, turn-arounds, increase, and advancement.

I know the Lord is doing that for people right now. Lift your hands and thank God that the latter half of your life will be better than the former half. God will give you a plan to receive double for everything that's been taken. You may have lost, but your days of losing are over.

Think of how the tide turned for Job. It was one loss after another, and then everything multiplied. When God gets involved, you'll go from not wanting to check the mail to fighting with your spouse over who *gets* to check the mail because it's always good news. I've always loved Billy Graham's ministry motto: "Always good news."

Blessings are flowing your way like waves of the ocean, one after another. God is restoring everything that was taken because you're His child. Life will not finish as it started. It's all because of Jesus!

Line your mouth up with the Bible, and you'll have continual victory. Start saying, "Today will be the lowest I'll ever be." The Lord will increase you a thousand times more—you and your descendants after you. God is a giver, and He is looking to increase you, in Jesus' name, but you must be born again.

Job feared the Lord and had nothing to do with evil. If you allow sin in your life, sin will put a hole in your hedge of protection and allow the enemy to come in. You must live a holy life. You'll be amazed how little spiritual warfare you'll have to engage in if you live a holy life. You'll be amazed how little you need prayer if you'll just kick sin out. Be what God admired about Job. *"He's an upright man, perfect in all his ways. He loves me and has nothing to do with evil."* You've got to be righteous. You can't cleanse your own hands, and you can't cleanse your own heart.

There's a hymn by William Cowper that says, "There is a fountain filled with blood, drawn from Immanuel's veins, that sinners who plunge beneath that flow lose all their guilty stains." Jesus will become your righteousness.

CHAPTER 16

SEVEN FACTS ABOUT APOSTLE PAUL

I'm writing this to help drive the religious thinking out of you. Religion causes people to view the Bible as a crutch or a tissue box to dry their eyes and blow their noses as they proceed to get their heads slapped around by the Devil all week. That's not the proper use of the Bible. The Bible says in Luke 10:19, *"Behold, I give you authority over all the power of the devil. You'll trample on snakes and scorpions, and nothing shall by any means harm you."* Jesus promised nothing would harm you. That's not hard to interpret. You can have protection against the enemy.

The Bible is an honest book. It's not like other religious texts that turn humans into mythological superheroes. The Bible tells you Paul was attacked. It tells you David committed adultery. The Bible recounts the time Elijah thought of taking his own life after he had just called fire down from Heaven. The challenges these men endured are biblical facts, but they are not doctrine. There's a difference between what the Bible recounts and doctrine. If the Bible tells you that Elisha was sick and died, that's not establishing a doctrine that you must die from sickness. It's telling you that Elisha was sick. It's that simple.

The Bible doesn't provide mixed messages. It's honest in its account of the lives of God's servants. It reveals that sometimes people miss the mark, but you can have what the Bible promises in Psalm 91.

Church history tells us that when John was boiled in oil, he didn't come out full of blisters and in need of an extended stay at a burn unit for skin grafts. Not only did he survive, but when they boiled him in oil, he emerged unscathed. The same thing happened when Shadrach, Meshach, and Abednego walked out of the fiery furnace—they weren't burned, and their hair and clothes didn't even smell like smoke. If these events happened today, they would happen in the same way. God hasn't changed; His promises have been upgraded based on our new covenant.

I want to use this chapter to address the life of Paul because his story often trips people up. God did not provide supernatural protection to His children in the Old Testament, just to give the Devil carte blanche in the New Testament after Jesus rose into Heaven and The Church was birthed, but that's how many people interpret the Bible. Let's review seven common misconceptions about Paul's life in this chapter and set the record straight.

1. Paul's Thorn in the Flesh

> Even though I have received such wonderful revelations from God. So to keep me from becoming proud, I was given a thorn in my flesh, a messenger from Satan to torment me and keep me from becoming proud. Three different times I begged the Lord to take it away. Each time he said, "My grace is all you need. My power works best in weakness." So now I am glad to boast about my weaknesses, so that the power of Christ can work through me. That's why I take pleasure in my weaknesses, and in the insults, hardships, persecutions, and troubles that I suffer for Christ. For when I am weak, then I am strong.
>
> — 2 CORINTHIANS 12:7-10

Paul's "thorn in the flesh" was not a caveat for sickness and disease to be put on you. Paul outlined his thorn in the verses above, and he never mentioned sickness or disease. He told you the thorn was a messenger sent from Satan to buffet him, to attack him blow after blow.

This has been happening to our ministry since we held our Festival of Life event. When people discovered what we were planning, they did their best to shut us down and even contacted people in a neighboring city to stir up trouble. It happened once again when we moved into our church building in Coraopolis, and our neighbors revoked their offer to provide us with additional parking. Then again, when we moved into Montour Junction and the city sent people to count heads and took us to court to have us illegally kicked out. Most recently, after being given thirty-six acres of property just in time for our *What No Eye Has Seen* camp meeting, members of the town tried to use the legal system to stop us from gathering. There have been people sent from Satan to attack us repeatedly, but our enemies can't persecute us by making anyone sick.

The "thorn in the flesh" is referred to as a personality. It appears multiple times throughout the Bible. It's always a person or a group of people, never a sickness or a disease. Paul cites people anointed by the Devil who did their best to stop his work, and he listed what they did—insult, persecute, cause hardship, and get him arrested. That's part of the Gospel. Jesus didn't remove you from the world; people will oppose you. People opposed Jesus, Peter, and Paul, but you cross the line when you allow persecution to affect you and your family with sickness, disease, or death because it violates Psalm 91.

2. Paul Knew Everything that Would Happen to Him

> Now there was a believer in Damascus named Ananias. The Lord spoke to him in a vision, calling, "Ananias!" "Yes, Lord!" he replied. The Lord said, "Go over to Straight Street, to the house of Judas. When you get there, ask for a man from Tarsus named Saul. He is praying to me right now. I have shown him a vision of a man named Ananias coming in and laying hands on him so he can see again." "But

Lord," exclaimed Ananias, "I've heard many people talk about the terrible things this man has done to the believers in Jerusalem! And he is authorized by the leading priests to arrest everyone who calls upon your name." But the Lord said, "Go, for Saul is my chosen instrument to take my message to the Gentiles and to kings, as well as to the people of Israel. And I will show him how much he must suffer for my name's sake."

— ACTS 9:10-16

Paul's suffering for the Gospel was not a surprise attack. Christ showed everything he would suffer in advance. If you claim Paul's suffering for you, your family, and your ministry, it could never be a surprise attack. You would have to tell people ahead of time.

Paul knew and made it known he was traveling to Rome to die. He knew exactly what would happen. Surprise attacks are not permitted in the Bible. God and Paul agreed that he would lay down his right of protection for the advancement of the Gospel.

3. Paul Didn't Die Until He Was Finished

As for me, my life has already been poured out as an offering to God. The time of my death is near. I have fought the good fight, I have finished the race, and I have remained faithful. And now the prize awaits me—the crown of righteousness, which the Lord, the righteous Judge, will give me on the day of his return. And the prize is not just for me but for all who eagerly look forward to his appearing.

— 2 TIMOTHY 4:6-8

The Devil didn't take Paul's life. Second Timothy is the last book of the Bible that the apostle Paul wrote, and in it he said, *"I have fought a good fight, I have finished the race, I have remained faithful. Now the prize awaits me."*

He told us his mission on Earth was complete. He was not taken out prematurely.

4. Paul Was Delivered from All His Persecutions

Anyone who portrays the Book of Acts in such a way that the persecutors defeated The Church is lying. That portrayal is not true.

> But you, Timothy, certainly know what I teach, and how I live, and what my purpose in life is. You know my faith, my patience, my love, and my endurance. You know how much persecution and suffering I have endured. You know all about how I was persecuted in Antioch, Iconium, and Lystra —but the Lord rescued me from all of it.
>
> — 2 TIMOTHY 3:10-11

Read and examine the specific persecutions Paul endured. When he was imprisoned, it wasn't a seventeen-year stint with the possibility of parole. He was out of prison in hours. God delivered him out of all the persecution and flipped it on the Devil. Bible scholars tell us that the jailer who arrested Paul washed his wounds and became the pastor of the church in Philippi. Not only did God deliver Paul from prison, He took what the Devil meant for evil and used it for good. That's the story of the Bible.

There is no acceptance of persecution for a life of defeat. Paul shook the known world with the Gospel to the point that even today, you can't travel anywhere without coming across a Saint Paul or São Paulo. Paul is everywhere. Is there any church where Paul's name isn't mentioned alongside Jesus'? He's forever linked with Christ. Two thousand years later, I'm still talking about him on YouTube. He wasn't defeated by the Devil. People tried to oppose him.

In Heaven, there'll be no opposition. On Earth, Jesus said there will be people who oppose you, but God gave you power to win and rule over them; they will not rule over you. *"Though the enemy comes in like a flood, the spirit of the Lord raises up a standard against it"* (Isaiah 59:19). That's the Bible, and there's no exception.

The Bible says one thing. It doesn't say multiple things. It doesn't tell you that God will beat down your foes before your face in Psalm 89 and claim your foes will beat you down in another. The Bible says you will *"rule thou in the midst of thy enemies"* (Psalm 110:2).

5. There is a Limitation on Persecution

> For our present troubles are small and won't last very long. Yet they produce for us a glory that vastly outweighs them and will last forever!
>
> — 2 CORINTHIANS 4:17

Our present troubles are small and won't last very long. Anything that moves beyond "momentary light affliction" has gone beyond what Paul said is permissible. You're not allowed to have large troubles, and you're not allowed to have trouble that lasts but for a moment.

Protestors threatened to kill me in Asbury Park, and the Department of Homeland Security was notified and became involved. They're no longer following me around. They're not stationed outside my home or the church. I was not beaten. I will never be beaten. There's a hedge of protection around me, my family, and everything I own.

6. Paul was Beaten

I'm not Paul. I'm with Christ. I'm not speaking against Paul, but the Bible does not say, "Looking unto Paul, the author and finisher of our faith." It says, *"ooking unto Jesus, the Author and Finisher of our faith."* Yes, Stephen was stoned to death, but again, Stephen is not the author and finisher of my faith. If you want to find people who were beaten and killed and make them your example, have at it. But scripturally, Christ is our example.

No one was able to lay a hand on Jesus until He laid down His life. One time His enemies tried to push Him over a cliff. Another time they tried to stone Him. He walked through a crowd, and no one dared lay a hand on Him. Even as He laid down His life, they came to arrest Him and Jesus said, *"Whom seek ye?"* And they said, *"Jesus of Nazareth."* He said, *"I am He,"* and they all fell to the ground backward. He knew they were coming and what they wanted, but He engaged them. Do you think He couldn't have gotten away?

No one could defeat Jesus until He laid His life down. The Bible teaches Christ is our example. Christ is the One I look to. No one was able to stop Jesus throughout His entire ministry on Earth. No one could lay a hand on Him. He experienced persecution, He was insulted, lied about, and betrayed. They did everything they could, but they still couldn't stop Him.

The Bible tells you in John 9 that anyone who claimed Jesus was the Messiah was no longer welcome in the synagogue. Imagine being banned from every church in the United States for embracing my ministry. That's persecution for the Gospel.

7. Paul was Imprisoned

In North America, it's illegal for you to be imprisoned for preaching the Gospel. How dumb do you have to be to cling to a story of someone being beaten and imprisoned when it's not even legal for that to happen to you? I didn't need supernatural intervention when people threatened to kill me. The Department of Homeland Security came on its own. If anyone approached me or crossed the street where I was preaching, they would have been arrested as soon as they set foot on the grass. You don't live in a nation where this stuff can happen, so why make it your doctrine?

The Bible is a book of victory. Quit trying to use it to justify your unemployment or failed marriage. Those are not examples of persecution; they're the product of a misunderstanding that you are more than a conqueror through Jesus Christ. As soon as that revelation enters your spirit, you'll stop being afflicted by the Devil and start afflicting the powers of darkness.

Why do Christians suffer so long? Why aren't instant deliverances common in the body of Christ? God backs up His Word with instant manifestations of His power.

I tell people, "Your season is coming." I preach, "You've put up with it enough. We're going to say one word, and the Devil will have to take his hands off your life for good." You get what you preach. You get what you believe. You get what you speak. When you believe for long hardship, you'll have long hardship. When you get a revelation that the finished work of Christ has eradicated the Devil's ability to take you out, then you go from glory to glory, victory to victory, and strength to strength.

You're free to believe what you want: momentary light afflictions or plagues of long continuance. Long-standing problems are listed as part of the curse of the law. You've suffered enough. God has no will for you to cry one more tear. In His presence is fullness of joy, not the fullness of suffering. At His right hand, pleasure forevermore. Don't expect to suffer; expect a miracle. Expect goodness and mercy to follow you all the days of your life.

It's not on God. It's on us. And it starts by having faith in your heart to declare it. Everything is as simple as what you believe and what you speak.

If you don't know the Lord, you won't have victory. Trouble chases sinners, while blessings chase the righteous. Everything starts with a commitment to give your life to Jesus Christ and turn your back on sin. This victory overcomes the world —even our faith.

CHAPTER 17

VISUALIZE YOUR VICTORY

> Now thanks be unto God, which always causeth us to triumph in Christ, and maketh manifest the savour of His knowledge by us in every place.
>
> — 2 CORINTHIANS 2:14 (KJV)

The triumph in this verse describes that of the Romans, in which a public and solemn honor was conferred upon a victorious general by allowing him a magnificent procession through the city of Rome. This was not granted by the Senate unless he had achieved a significant and decisive victory or conquered a province. On such occasions, the general was clad in purple and gold, figured and adorned, setting forth his achievements. He wore a crown and, in one hand, held a branch of laurel: the emblem of victory. He carried his staff. He rode a magnificent chariot adorned with ivory and plates of gold and drawn by white horses. To keep him humble amid all this, a slave rode at his back, casting reproaches and railings, enumerating his vices and failures. Musicians led the procession. Young men led animal sacrifices to be offered. Then came loads of spoil, followed by the kings, princes, and generals taken captive. After these came the triumphal chariot, before which people spread flowers and shouted, "Triumph in Christ!" Following this came the Senate priests and the rest of the parade. Triumph in Christ means complete mastery over satanic powers.[i]

That's how the Bible says we're to go through life on Earth. Like the generals on their triumphal procession through the city of Rome after they'd conquered in battle. That's how we're being led by Christ in triumph. He leads us in triumph in *this* life.

> My child, listen to me and do as I say, and you will have a long, good life. I will teach you wisdom's ways and lead you in straight paths. When you walk, you won't be held back; when you run, you won't stumble. Take hold of my instructions; don't let them go. Guard them, for they are the key to life. Don't do as the wicked do, and don't follow the path of evildoers. Don't even think about it; don't go that way. Turn away and keep moving. For evil people can't sleep until they've done their evil deed for the day. They can't rest until they've caused someone to stumble. They eat the food of wickedness and drink the wine of violence! The way of the righteous is like the first gleam of dawn, which shines ever brighter until the full light of day.
>
> — PROVERBS 4:10-18

> But the path of the just is as the shining light, that shineth more and more unto the perfect day.
>
> — PROVERBS 4:18 (KJV)

In verse 18, we see the bright and luminous path of the just. This proves that at death, the righteous one does not go into a dormant, unconscious state until the resurrection, but their path gets brighter and brighter until he emerges into the full blaze of endless glory.[ii]

The Bible teaches that the path of the righteous is akin to how the sunlight breaks at dawn. The sun doesn't go up and down in the morning; it shines brighter and brighter until the full light of day. That's what the path of the righteous is likened to. You continue to shine brighter and brighter until you go to see Jesus. That's the path we're on.

> The Lord is my shepherd; I shall not want. He maketh me to lie down in green pastures: He leadeth me beside the still waters.
>
> — PSALM 23:1-2 (KJV)

The doctrine of supplying lawful wants and needs is taught in both testaments.[iii] God doesn't only supply your needs, He supplies your wants and needs as long as they're in line with the law of God. The comfort of the Shepherd's rod and staff are for His sheep. They are the only two items shepherds carry for defense and help. The club is for the sheep's enemies, and the crook is for the sheep's protection.[iv]

If you take these verses to heart, nothing can stand against you. Get all the religion out of your spirit that teaches you to expect defeat from time to time or seasons of hardship. The Bible doesn't just teach victory, the Bible teaches continual victory—victory after victory. Not mountains and valleys. Always the head, never the tail. Always on top, never at the bottom.

> "I have told you these things, so that in Me you may have [perfect] peace and confidence. In the world you have tribulation and trials and distress and frustration; but be of good cheer [take courage; be confident, certain, undaunted]! For I have overcome the world. [I have deprived it of power to harm you and have conquered it for you]."
>
> — JOHN 16:33 (AMPC)

This is a scripture people often cite when attempting to argue against our covenant right to live in continuous victory. The first part of the verse does speak of trials and tribulations, but the presence of a trial does not constitute defeat. If you continue reading, it goes on to say that

God has overcome the world and robbed it of any power to harm you. Jesus conquered the world for you.

We've read chapter after chapter that promises victory. It's not an interpretation of the Bible; it's what the Bible teaches. There is no dichotomy in the Bible. It doesn't teach that you can have victory and then also teach you must suffer defeat. The suffering the Bible refers to is rejection by the world. It's described from the perspective of Heaven. In Heaven, you won't have people yelling at you and giving you the middle finger for speaking God's Word. Those are things that the Bible considers suffering, not being beaten and bloody or your child dying. That's not it. Suffering in the Bible refers to the opposition to the advancement of the Gospel.

> No, despite all these things, overwhelming victory is ours through Christ, who loved us.
>
> — ROMANS 8:37

We must conclude from these doctrines that God is for us and will freely give us all things. We learn that God alone is our Judge, that Christ and the Holy Spirit are our helpers, that nothing can separate us from the love of Christ, and that we are more than conquerors over all enemies through Jesus Christ our Lord.[v]

> Who are kept by the power of God through faith unto salvation ready to be revealed in the last time. Wherein ye greatly rejoice, though now for a season, if need be, ye are in heaviness through manifold temptations: That the trial of your faith, being much more precious than of gold that perisheth, though it be tried with fire, might be found unto praise and honour and glory at the appearing of Jesus Christ.
>
> — 1 PETER 1:5-7 (KJV)

The trial of your faith will make your faith as pure as gold. In practical terms that means when the head of permits denies your request, you obtain the permit by faith. That victory causes your faith to become refined like gold. You may feel you have faith, but when you stand against a Goliath, a fiery furnace, or a lion's den, it *proves* your faith. It doesn't give you faith to go through a trial, it purifies your faith.

The next time you're confronted by an enemy, you know you've already won the victory. You can say, like David, *"The God that delivered me out of the paw of the lion and the paw of the bear will deliver me from this Philistine."* When the lions, giants, or storms come, their purpose is not to defeat or afflict you but to purify your faith and provide you with the confidence to win your next battle.

> Once we were safe on shore, we learned that we were on the island of Malta. The people of the island were very kind to us. It was cold and rainy, so they built a fire on the shore to welcome us. As Paul gathered an armful of sticks and was laying them on the fire, a poisonous snake, driven out by the heat, bit him on the hand. The people of the island saw it hanging from his hand and said to each other, "A murderer, no doubt! Though he escaped the sea, justice will not permit him to live." But Paul shook off the snake into the fire and was unharmed.
>
> — ACTS 28:1-5

The snake is part of this world. You will not have to put up with him in Heaven. It bit Paul's hand, but it didn't kill him. He didn't swell up, or even fight it off. He immediately shook it off into the fire. That's New Testament suffering.

> The people waited for him to swell up or suddenly drop dead. But when they had waited a long time and saw that he wasn't harmed, they changed their minds and decided he was a god.
>
> — ACTS 28:6

When you face problems, it should reveal to others that you carry God in your mortal flesh, even unsaved people should be able to tell you're different.

> Near the shore where we landed was an estate belonging to Publius, the chief official of the island. He welcomed us and treated us kindly for three days. As it happened, Publius's father was ill with fever and dysentery. Paul went in and prayed for him, and laying his hands on him, he healed him. Then all the other sick people on the island came and were healed. As a result we were showered with honors, and when the time came to sail, people supplied us with everything we would need for the trip.
>
> — ACTS 28:7-10

In the original language, when it says, *"We were showered with gifts,"* it means high-honor gifts. Paul was shipwrecked, and within a handful of days, he was staying at the governor's mansion, and everyone on the island was showering him with gifts.

If I had to run a 26-mile marathon and I was given one billion dollars for finishing, you would not hear me talking about how hard it was to run the 26 miles when one billion dollars was put into my account. Why do people choose to focus on the snake bite? How do you focus on the shipwreck when it ends with Paul in the governor's mansion and everyone on the island showering him with gifts? Challenges are a normal part of life, but it's unscriptural to be defeated. Receive that into your spirit today, in Jesus' name.

AFTERWORD

When you get saved, you're reborn as a new creation. You're redeemed into an enviable destiny that empowers you to prevail in every battle of life.

This book is a roadmap to prosperity and success in everything you do. The Bible is not filled with arbitrary rules God gave us for fun, they lead to a victorious destination. God told us that if we apply His instructions, He will give us success and prosperity in everything we do. The Holy Spirit never leads to failure.

God always leads forward. God doesn't take people down—He takes them up. He takes the beggar from the dunghill and sets him among princes (1 Samuel 2:8). That's the God I serve. That's the God I'm telling you about. He doesn't want you to walk aimlessly through life in hopes that one day it'll all be worth it when we get to Heaven—He wants you to **prevail.**

Success is not automatic; we must pursue it. *"Meditate on My Word day and night."* Take it seriously as a matter of life and death. Stay in the Bible morning and night. Set aside time to read it and let the Bible point out flaws in your life. Pursue success and grab it by faith. Not a faith that survives, not a faith that comforts you during the storm, but faith that

AFTERWORD

prevails and takes ground for the Kingdom of God. This is the faith I'm imparting to you, in Jesus' name.

If you don't know the Lord, you won't prevail. *"Trouble chases sinners, blessings chase the righteous"* (Proverbs 13:21). Everything starts with a commitment to turn your life toward Jesus Christ and turn your back on sin. *"Whoever is born of God overcomes the world, and this is the victory that overcomes the world, even our faith."* Until God's seed is in you, until you're born again, you don't have the power to prevail in every battle because His power is not in you.

You may read this book, and if you're honest with yourself, you can't point to a time when you ever prayed the prayer of salvation. You're living a life of default. Maybe you've fallen away and are now far from God, but you're ready to recommit your life to the Lord and KNOW that you're saved. The Revival Today Staff is available to pray with you. Call the number below to talk to a real person who cares about you and will pray with and for you. It's the most important decision you will ever make!

Call 412-787-2578

It's normal to be challenged; it's unscriptural to be defeated. Receive that into your spirit today. You can prevail over every battle of life, in Jesus' name.

NOTES

CHAPTER 9

i. Dake, F. J. (2014). *Dake's annotated reference Bible: the Holy Bible, containing the Old and New Testaments of the Authorized or King James version text.* http://ci.nii.ac.jp/ncid/BA60156045
ii. Ibid, 305.

CHAPTER 10

i. Ibid, 114.
ii. Ibid, 1149.

CHAPTER 12

i. Ibid, 79.
ii. Ibid.

CHAPTER 14

i. Hillhouse, T. M., & Porter, J. H. (2015). A brief history of the development of antidepressant drugs: from monoamines to glutamate. *Experimental and clinical psychopharmacology, 23*(1), 1–21.

CHAPTER 17

i. Dake, Finis Jennings. *Dake's annotated reference Bible: the Holy Bible, containing the Old and New Testaments of the Authorized or King James version text.* 2014, ci.nii.ac.jp/ncid/BA60156045.
ii. Ibid, 1067.
iii. Ibid, 920.
iv. Ibid.
v. Ibid, 292.

"My generation shall be saved!"

— JONATHAN SHUTTLESWORTH

ABOUT THE AUTHOR

Evangelist and Pastor, Jonathan Shuttlesworth, is the founder of Revival Today and Pastor of Revival Today Church, ministries dedicated to reaching lost and hurting people with The Gospel of Jesus Christ.

In fulfilling his calling, Jonathan Shuttlesworth has conducted meetings and open-air crusades throughout North America, India, the Caribbean, and Central and South Africa.

Revival Today Church was launched in 2022 as a soul-winning, Holy Spirit-honoring church that is unapologetic about believing the Bible to bless families and nations.

Each day thousands of lives are impacted globally through Revival Today Broadcasting and Revival Today Church, located in Pittsburgh, PA; Fort Worth, TX; Los Angeles, CA; and Phoenix, AZ.

While methods may change, Revival Today's heartbeat remains for the lost, providing biblical teaching on faith, healing, prosperity, freedom from sin, and living a victorious life.

If you need help or would like to partner with Revival Today to see this generation and nation transformed through The Gospel, follow these links...

www.RevivalToday.com
www.RevivalTodayChurch.com

Get access to our 24/7 network Revival Today Global Broadcast. Download the Revival Today app in your Apple App Store or Google Play Store. Watch live on Apple TV, Roku, Amazon Fire TV, and Android TV.

Call: 412-787-2578

facebook.com/revivaltoday
x.com/jdshuttlesworth
instagram.com/jdshuttlesworth
youtube.com/@jonathanshuttlesworth

DO SOMETHING TODAY THAT WILL CHANGE YOUR LIFE FOREVER

THUS SAITH THE LORD, **MAKE THIS VALLEY FULL OF DITCHES.** FOR THUS SAITH THE LORD, YE SHALL NOT SEE WIND, NEITHER SHALL YE SEE RAIN; YET THAT VALLEY SHALL BE FILLED WITH WATER... **THIS IS BUT A LIGHT THING IN THE SIGHT OF THE LORD**... AND IT CAME TO PASS... **THE COUNTRY WAS FILLED WITH WATER.**
2 KINGS 3:16-18; 20

Revival is the only answer to the problems of this country - nothing more, nothing less, nothing else.

Thank you for standing with me as a partner with Revival Today. We must see this nation shaken by the power of God.

You cannot ask God to bless you first, prior to giving. God asks you to step out first in your giving - and then He makes it rain. We are believing God for 1,000 people to partner with us monthly at $84. Something everyone can do, but a significant seed that will connect you to the rainmaker.

IF YOU HAVE NOT YET PARTNERED WITH REVIVAL TODAY, JOIN US TODAY!

This year is not your year **to dig small ditches.** When I grew tired of small meetings and altar calls, I moved forward in faith and God responded. God is the rainmaker, but you must give Him something to fill. It's time for you to move forward! **Will you stand with me today to see the nations of the world shaken by the power of God?**

Revivaltoday.com/give

revivaltoday.com/paypal

Zelle® info@revivaltoday.com

 @RTgive

Text "GIVE" to 75767
Call at (412) 787-2578

Mail a check to:

Revival Today P.O. BOX 7
PROSPERITY PA 15329

REVIVAL TODAY   Email: info@revivaltoday.com

www.ingramcontent.com/pod-product-compliance
Lightning Source LLC
Chambersburg PA
CBHW021157160426
43194CB00007B/778